Congratulations on your new book. It sounds fascinating and we look forward to reading it. That is a "hot topic" right now.

—CAPT. DALE AND PAULA BLACK,
AUTHORS OF *FLIGHT TO HEAVEN*
AND *LIFE, CANCER AND GOD*

The choice of your book cover sent shivers down my spine. Michele, I can't wait to read your book.

—BRENDA (A MESSIANIC JEW),
ISLE OF WIGHT, UK

THE END OF THE WORLD

OF THE

WORLD

And What **Jesus** Has to Say About It

MICHELE NEAL

CREATION HOUSE

THE END OF THE WORLD, AND WHAT JESUS HAS TO SAY ABOUT IT
by Michele Neal
Published by Creation House
A Charisma Media Company
600 Rinehart Road
Lake Mary, Florida 32746
www.charismamedia.com

Unless otherwise indicated, all scripture quotations are taken from the Holy Bible, New Living Translation, copyright © 1996, 2004, 2007 by Tyndale House Foundation. Used by permission of Tyndale House Publishers, Inc., Carol Stream, Illinois 60188. All rights reserved.

Scripture quotations marked KJV are from the King James Version of the Bible.

Scripture quotations marked NIV are from the Holy Bible, New International Version. Copyright © 1973, 1978, 1984, 2010, 2011, International Bible Society. Used by permission.

Scripture quotations marked NKJV are from the New King James Version of the Bible. Copyright © 1979, 1980, 1982 by Thomas Nelson, Inc., publishers. Used by permission.

Publisher's Note: The views expressed in this book are not necessarily the views held by the publisher.

Design Director: Bill Johnson
Cover design by Terry Clifton

Visit the author's websites: www.theendoftheworld.uk.com and www.comeonchurchwakeup.com.

Library of Congress CataloginginPublication Data: 2014902931
International Standard Book Number: 978-1-62136-742-0
E-book International Standard Book Number: 978-1-62136-743-7

While the author has made every effort to provide accurate telephone numbers and Internet addresses at the time of publication, neither the publisher nor the author assumes any responsibility for errors or for changes that occur after publication.

First edition

14 15 16 17 — 9 8 7 6 5 4 3 2 1

Printed in Canada

DEDICATION

I dedicate this book to my heavenly Father,
His Son, Jesus Christ, and to the Holy Spirit.

The message of this book is from the Word
of God. I am simply the hand that He is using to write it. It has been a long and hard
work, and I claim no glory or credit for
myself. My sole purpose is to obey the
Lord in what He has led me to write.

I would not write this book unless the Lord
had laid upon my heart the urgency of His
Word concerning the second coming of
His Son, Jesus Christ, and the approaching end of the world, with the overwhelming burden to wake up the body of believers who have fallen into a deep slumber.

Only God is worthy of all the glory and all the
praise, because it is His message to both believers and unbelievers. I am just the messenger
being called upon to deliver His message.

To God be the glory!

The Sovereign LORD has spoken—so who can refuse to proclaim His message?

—AMOS 3:8

Those who speak for themselves want glory for themselves, but a person who seeks to honor the one who sent him speaks truth, not lies.

—JOHN 7:18

Be careful that you do not refuse to listen to the One who is speaking. For if the people of Israel did not escape when they refused to listen to Moses, the earthly messenger, we will certainly not escape if we reject the One who speaks to us from heaven!

—HEBREWS 12:25

Then the angel said to me, "Everything you have heard and seen is trustworthy and true. The Lord God, who inspires His prophets, has sent His angel *to tell His servants what will happen soon.*"

—REVELATION 22:6, EMPHASIS ADDED

Look, I am coming soon! Blessed are those who obey the words of prophecy written in this book.

—REVELATION 22:7

"Look, I am coming soon, bringing my reward with me to repay all people according to their deeds. I am the Alpha and the Omega, the First and the Last, the Beginning and the End." Blessed are those who wash their robes. They will be permitted to enter through the gates of the city and eat the fruit from the tree of life. Outside the city are the dogs—the sorcerers, the sexually immoral, the murderers, the idol worshipers, *and all who love to live a lie.*

—REVELATION 22:12–15, EMPHASIS ADDED

O earth, earth, earth, hear the word of the LORD.

—JEREMIAH 22:29

ACKNOWLEDGMENTS

OVER THE PAST eighteen months, since the completion of my first book, *Come on Church! Wake Up!*, so many people have joined me on this journey. Thank you to absolutely everyone who has read my first book and has taken hold of Jesus' message, and is now running with it and reaching out to others with its message. You are all wonderful people and are all a part of God's work in this urgent ministry. I may never meet you all or get to know you personally on Earth, but I pray we will all meet in heaven when Jesus returns for His bride.

Certain people I know personally have supported me in prayer and friendship during the writing of both books; and I would like to thank all of you, for without your faithful encouragement over tea and cake and through your e-mails and Facebook, I might have given up under the burden. Thank you for underpinning me with your Christlike love. I pray that your reward in heaven will be abundant!

Thank you to the wonderful brothers and sisters in Christ that the Lord has brought into our lives since we moved to the Isle of Wight in August 2013 and to the staff and members of the church we now attend. Your friendship, prayers, encouragement, and support are such a blessing to us in the work that we are now undertaking for the kingdom of God. May the Lord bless you all in more ways than you could ever imagine!

Thank you to those involved in the creation and running of my websites and IT support. I really do appreciate the skills the Lord has blessed you with.

Also, unending thanks to my twin sister, Sharon, my precious daughter, Emma, and my forever long-suffering husband, Chris, for cheering me on through the tough stuff when I felt like lying down and never getting up again!

To Creation House Publishers, a huge thank you for all that you have done to get my first book out into the "big wide world"! The last time I looked it was available on over two hundred and fifty different websites all around the globe! Praise and glory to the Lord for the gifts He has given all the Creation House team to be able to spread His Word around the world!

Finally, a big thank you to everyone who has "liked" my Facebook page and posted comments on it and to everyone who has visited my website: www.comeonchurchwakeup.com.

You have all strengthened and encouraged me immensely! What would I do without your friendship in Christ? Thank you all for your willing and loving hearts. God bless you all!

CONTENTS

FOREWORD

MICHELE NEAL IS a remarkable lady who puts Jesus first in all she does; including her own health. In the short period of time I have been her minister, I am amazed by the depth of her spirituality. She reflects on deeply profound theological insights in everyday language at a level all can engage with. Michele's great skill with this is evidenced within her books; she seems able to speak these deep spiritual truths to us and then unpacks them for us to understand.

Having read Michele's first book, *Come on Church! Wake Up!: Sin Within the Church and What Jesus Has to Say About It*, as a church we have been awakened to the seriousness of sin within the church and we now sit bolt upright to the issues we face in these end times.

Michele skillfully opens our minds to what Jesus says within the Gospels, as well as what the apostles and prophets say, and finally what John says within the Book of Revelation about the impact of the end of the world for believers and unbelievers alike. Her insight into the Scriptures wakes us up to the reality of the times we live in and how we need to draw closer to the truths of the Bible.

Michele seems to bear in her body the spiritual burden of waking up the church to the truth of God's Word. She is often in pain or feels fatigued, but the biggest blessing is to see her worshiping. She will dance around like a teenager waving colored banners and flags, free of pain and full of energy, as she is totally free in her heavenly Father's presence. As she has struggled physically to write this book, what has carried her through is the presence of God in her life. In her physical weakness it is His strength that has enabled her to bring the realities of *The End of the World* into our everyday understanding.

I am very proud to know Michele and her family. It's a great blessing for me to support and encourage her as well as endorse this book to you. I wish you wisdom and every blessing in how you use this reflection on this inspiring book and person.

—REV. MARK J. EVANS, BTH (OXON), MINISTER
NEWPORT CONGREGATIONAL CHURCH,
ISLE OF WIGHT

TESTIMONY

BEFORE I WRITE about the subject of this book, I would like to share with you as briefly as I can the testimony about the events surrounding the publishing of my first book, *Come on Church! Wake Up!* It is nothing short of miraculous, and is a hugely eventful, moving, and nail-biting journey that the Lord took me on from beginning to end!

The testimony of the dramatic events that caused that book to come into being has already been written in that book, so I won't retell that story here. What I would like to share with you now is what happened prior to the publishing of it and its journey up to the supply of books arriving at my front door.

The first miracle occurred from the moment I picked up my pen to begin writing the manuscript at the end of October 2011. I had suddenly and mysteriously become very ill and was in intense pain and unable to eat anything. Even trying to drink something was an ordeal, yet I was overwhelmed by the power of the Holy Spirit, who took me through a period of revealing to me the state of my unrepentant sinful life as a believer. During that time the Holy Spirit enabled me to handwrite the draft manuscript for my first book from my sick bed. That 35,000 word draft was completed in two weeks, which is something I could never have achieved in my own strength, even if I had been fully well.

After completing the handwritten manuscript in that intense and short period of time, I felt exhausted by all that the Lord had taken me through. The draft was done, but I needed time to recover from the experience. Several months went by as I slowly got myself back in to some sort of "normal" routine; all the while the draft manuscript sat there silently calling my attention. I could hear the Holy Spirit whispering to me, "Do the manuscript. Do the manuscript," but "life" kept getting in the way.

I kept making excuses not to carry on with it, telling myself that I couldn't possibly have a book published about sin within the church, and what Jesus has to say about it. I could hear voices in my mind sniggering at me, saying, "Who on earth do you think you are writing a book like this? Everyone will think you are some sort of self-righteous prig! You don't seriously think that God has called you to speak out a message like this, do you? You are completely crazy!"

At one point I nearly gave up due to the huge bombarding feelings of doubt and fear. To be truthful, I was actually terrified. Apart from my husband, daughter, and sister, I could not tell anyone about what had happened to me, as I didn't think they would believe me. I felt like I was at a great crossroads in my life and absolutely no one could help me. I had a decision to make: either stay stuck where I was with a manuscript hidden forever out of sight in a drawer, *or* believe that the Lord had called me to write it through a very painful personal experience, submit it to the publisher, and trust God with the outcome of it.

At that very difficult time, the Lord sent one of His "ministering angels" to shine a light on the path that He wanted me to take. In January 2012, a very precious word from the Lord was given by a member of the church we attended. It had been printed in the church newsletter; and when I read it, I wept silent tears of thanksgiving to the Lord for seeing my great dilemma, hearing my cry for help, and faithfully providing the answer.

Below is the word that was given, which I share with every reader with the permission of the person, who wishes to remain anonymous, whom the Lord used to speak His message. As you read it, I pray that it will minister to you in the same powerful way that it ministered to me.

THE LORD BELIEVES IN YOU

I feel the Lord is saying, "I believe in you." The seed of a dream that is beginning to germinate in your heart has been planted there by the Lord. As the shoots are beginning to form, the enemy is seeking to choke its growth and destroy it before it can come to fruition.

You have been listening to words from various sources seeking to tear you down, to have you think that this dream is not of the Lord, that you have misheard, that you are not capable of fulfilling it, that you will fail. Will you keep paying attention to the negative report or will you receive the affirming word of the Lord?

He comes to reassure you that the promise and the vision are from Him. He knows your potential and what you are capable of achieving as you discover the giftings and abilities He has placed within you. He will be your teacher, your counselor, your wisdom, and your strength. Under His guiding and His anointing you will succeed if you are willing to place yourself in His hands and be trained, prepared, and released for His purposes to be fulfilled in and through you. Others may doubt you, you may doubt yourself; but the Lord says, "I believe in you."

This powerful message acted as the dynamite of the Holy Spirit and blasted me into action! I knew that the Lord was speaking to me, and at that precise moment all the lies of the enemy were silenced.

After many months of proofreading the manuscript and making any necessary corrections, I was ready to submit it to Creation House Publishers. I had only once made a general inquiry to them about potential financial matters to do with publishing a book, but with no definite indication as to when a manuscript might be submitted for their consideration.

Six months after the first drafting of the manuscript, I felt an overwhelming insistence inside me urging me to send the manuscript urgently. This insistence was so strong and I believed it was a powerful prompting of the Lord, so I decided to tell my husband that the following day (April 24, 2012), I absolutely *had* to submit the manuscript to the publisher and that I was not going to go to bed that night until it had been submitted. I would like to point out that the publisher had no idea about any of this.

So on the evening of April 24, 2012, we switched on the computer and I opened up the e-mails. As I sat there scanning through the inbox, there on the screen was a message I will never forget for the rest of my life. The message in my inbox was from Creation House Publishers. The title of the message said, "Michele; It is time to publish your book!" I sat there with my heart pounding and tears streaming silently down my face.

What are the chances of these words appearing "at random" in an e-mail from the publisher on the *exact* day and at the *exact* moment that I am about to send the manuscript to them; and without them even knowing that I was sitting at the computer about to submit it?

All the previous doubts that I had had as to whether the writing of that book was from the Lord were blasted away by the message on the screen. My eyes were fixed on the message, and I felt that God was speaking to me directly through those words to reassure me that the manuscript I was about to submit was definitely His work. Despite this reassurance, clicking the "submit" button was a very difficult thing to do. I did not do it lightly. My husband and I prayed as I sent it, and we committed the outcome of it into God's hands.

The publisher's FAQs stated that it may take up to three months to hear from them as to whether a manuscript has been accepted or not, so I was not concerned in the slightest during the following three months. I just waited patiently with the peace of the Lord surrounding me and carried on with my daily life as a housewife and mother.

Then exactly three months after I had submitted it, I felt the Lord prompt me to contact the publisher to find out what the situation was. I sent them an e-mail and received a reply within minutes. They said that they had replied to my manuscript submission in April, *seven days* after I had sent it, offering me a contract. But I had not received that e-mail at the end of April 2012. I believe that the three-month delay was an attack of Satan in the spiritual realm to hold up the work of the Lord.

I received a new proposal from the publisher in July 2012 and signed the contract a month later. But at the precise moment that I was about to submit the signed contract to them by e-mail, our computer was hit by a virus, which caused it to crash, leaving it unusable for four days. I was not about to let Satan think he had gotten any sort of victory, so I rang the publisher in Florida to let them know what had happened and to inform them that the contract was now making its way to them from the UK by airmail.

All went more or less smoothly between August and November 2012. Then at the critical point of my personal consignment of a thousand books leaving the printing firm in Canada, things began to go a bit strange. I had been told by the freight company that my shipment would be on a flight from Toronto airport in early December and that they would contact us on its arrival at Heathrow airport to arrange delivery to our house.

Five days later, having heard nothing further, we contacted them and discovered that for some reason my consignment had been taken off the flight. So it was rebooked on a flight a whole week later. I was given the flight number. The morning that it was due to land, I sat at my computer and entered the flight number into the flight tracker; like an excited child, I watched it land at Heathrow on the computer screen. We all rejoiced and then waited patiently for a call from the freight company to arrange delivery. Having received no call, we rang them the following day only to discover that *again*, my shipment of books had been removed from the flight. So they rebooked it on that evening's flight and assured us that it would definitely be on that one.

I decided that I was not going to even think about it anymore and was definitely not going to watch the new flight on the flight tracker the next day. I handed the whole matter over to my capable husband, while I got on with my other role in life—doing the housework!

As the day that the consignment was due to land was a Saturday and both the freight company office and the customs office at the airport were closed over the weekend, we had to wait until the following Monday to find out if it had actually arrived. On that Monday we did receive the long-awaited phone call to say the books had landed safely and were awaiting clearance through customs; they would be delivered the next day.

The following morning I kept looking out the window for the delivery van to arrive. When it eventually did, I walked outside; and as the driver opened the doors of his van, I burst into tears when I saw my boxes of books. He looked at me, a bit unsure of what to make of my emotional outburst. So I explained to him that he had a very special consignment on his van and that he was playing an extremely important part in fulfilling a long-awaited vision. He seemed quite touched by this, so I proceeded to tell him what the cargo was that he was delivering and gave him a promotional leaflet my sister had produced which explained what the book was about.

In early 2010, when the Lord first impressed upon me the message to wake up the church and to write a book, I had absolutely no idea what He wanted me to write. All I had were the words He spoke deep into my soul, which were, "Wake up, church!" I felt that this was to be the original title of the book. The draft manuscript was handwritten with that title, and it was also typed up with that title. I have kept these as evidence.

Shortly before I submitted the manuscript to the publisher, I began to feel uneasy about the title, even though the Lord had given me the words, "Wake up, Church!" back in the early part of 2010. I was really quite anxious about this uneasy feeling because I didn't want to just change the title without His confirmation. But I kept feeling an insistence inside me saying, "You must change the title." I realized that this was the Holy Spirit prompting me to change it, even though I had no idea why. A new title kept coming into my mind: *Come on Church! Wake Up!* So I changed the title, submitted it to the publisher, and that is the title of the published book.

Shortly after its official release in January 2013, while I was searching the Internet for its availability, I noticed a few websites saying, "Wake up, Church!" I could hardly believe my eyes! So I clicked on one of them to see what it was about. To my utter amazement, a book by another author, Greg Wilburn, had been published in October 2010 with that very title.

At that very moment, I understood why the Lord had created an insistence inside me to change the title of my own book before submitting it to the publisher. The Lord already knew that the original title He had given to me had now been used by another servant of His, and that I could not submit my manuscript with the same title. Although, at the time, I did not know what the reason was for the need to change the title of my book, I had to believe that the insistence that I felt was from God, obey that insistence, and trust in God that He knew what the reason was.

How absolutely amazing is our God! It seems He is certainly using other believers to get the message out that His church needs to wake up.

Since my first book's release in January 2013, I have watched its online availability grow from one website to currently over 250 websites all around the world (as of March 2014).

So that is it in as short a testimony as I can make it. I am so thankful to God for pulling me through it all, and I give Him all the praise and all the glory for the future outcome of the work that He asked me to undertake for His kingdom.

And now begins my second book. As you read this, I pray that the Lord will speak to you through each page. It is His message concerning the end of the world, and what Jesus has to say about it. It is a vital message for the perplexing times we are now living in.

May God's message do a mighty work within all who profess to be followers of Christ, to make you truly ready for the day of Jesus' return.

Chapter 1
THE REASON FOR THIS BOOK

*But the day of the Lord will come like a thief. The heavens
will disappear with a roar; the elements will be destroyed
by fire, and the earth and everything in it will be laid bare.
Since everything will be destroyed in this way, what kind of
people ought you to be? You ought to live holy and godly lives
as you look forward to the day of God and speed its coming.*

—2 Peter 3:10–12, niv

I F YOU DO an Internet search for "end times" or "the end of the
world," you will be overwhelmed with what meets your eyes.
However, much of what is available to read and watch is often
based on a secular and nonbiblical viewpoint. It would appear
that millions of people around the world are interested in what
appears to be one of the hottest topics of the century, all searching
for answers and even specific dates for when the world will end.

The purpose of this book is to focus on what Jesus has to say
about the end of the world in accordance with what is written in
the Holy Bible. I will also record what some of the apostles have
said about this extremely important matter to fellow believers, as
well as identifying some of the Old Testament prophecies concerning the end of the world which were spoken by the prophets
prior to Jesus' first coming more than 2,000 years ago.

The chapter regarding the words of the apostles will demonstrate
that they believed what Jesus said concerning the end times and
the signs that would indicate the approaching end, which they

1

duly taught to the believers as the truth, exhorting them to be diligent in their observation and discernment of occurring events.

The chapter relating to the prophets will show that God chose them to be His voice to the world, and their prophecies continue to warn us that the world will end at an appointed time. The Old Testament prophecies were not all "time specific" to apply to the days before Jesus first came. Many of the prophecies are warnings relating to the future end of the world and are applicable to an era or generation that will remain in existence when the end-time signs begin to unfold on an ever increasing scale.

God has warned us of the end of the world throughout the Old Testament; Jesus has warned us of its impending reality throughout the New Testament; and the apostles have upheld the truth of this message in their letters and epistles to believers. Clearly the end of the world is going to happen. God has *not* changed His mind on this! The end of the world as we know it is the culmination and fulfillment of His eternal plan, and it *will* come to pass. God's Word says that no one will know when the end will be; not the angels, not even Jesus Himself, but only God (see Matthew 24:36; Mark 13:32).

This book will clearly show what Jesus says will be the signs and evidence of His approaching return, which will hasten in the end of the world. In view of this, perhaps it would be wise to open our eyes and our ears and look at what is happening around us in the heavens, on the earth, and in the sea and weigh up our observations to see if the visible evidence is confirmed in the holy Word of God. As God has said that He will bring the world to an end, we cannot afford to continue living a narrow-minded lifestyle, with our heads buried in the sand, ignoring the glaringly obvious signs all around us, pretending all is well in our little world.

All is *far* from well! And our little world is groaning and struggling under the strain of the sin and evil that mankind is inflicting upon it. The earth is demonstrating its distress with outward visible signs of destruction, devastation, catastrophe, and collapse on an escalating scale approaching cataclysmic proportions.

In the past two years, the Lord has opened my eyes to the unfolding signs of the end times. Despite being a born-again, Spirit-filled believer for over twenty-one years, I failed to believe that any end-time events could actually occur in our lifetime. I merely assumed that they would occur at some future point in time, long after I had drawn my last breath. I have spent much of my Christian life with total disregard to the scriptural exhortation to discern events in relation to the end times. I have to confess that I had been wrapped up in my own life until October 2011 when the Lord began to cause me to "see."

About four years ago, when the Lord gave me the words "wake up, church!" which brought about the writing of my first book, *Come on Church! Wake Up!*, the Lord also gave me the words "the unveiling of revelation." At the end of each year, I come before the Lord in prayer and ask Him if He would impress upon me His word for the new year ahead, and the words "the unveiling of revelation" were given in relation to the year 2010.

Since that time, I have sought the Lord at each New Year for His description of where things are at from a global perspective. For 2011, the description given was "death and destruction," and for 2012, the description the Lord gave was "cataclysmic collapse." Throughout 2012 I watched with silent shock as the global news unfolded on a daily basis. The events in the news were frequently described as times of unprecedented collapse, not just financially but also nationally, socially, morally, and relationally. I frequently did Internet searches for "end times" throughout 2012, and a great many of the listings were headed "Global Collapse 2012." It is as if the earth has finally had enough and is beginning to display the signs of end-time collapse.

The word the Lord gave me for 2013 was "escalation." As I type this page, it is the beginning of April 2013. The amount of escalation of global collapse and other devastating events that I have witnessed around the world in the first three months of 2013 is truly shocking. It is almost beyond belief.

By the time this book is published, halfway through 2014, I am certain that a tremendous amount of escalation will have occurred during that time.

END-TIME DREAMS

I often wonder why the Lord gives me vivid words concerning each year ahead. They are a very heavy burden to bear, and I have been left wondering what God wants me to do with the descriptions He has given me. But I have noticed over the past three years, as He has given me each description, I have increasingly had what I can only describe as vivid end-time dreams. I did not have these before 2010; but once I started having them, they increased from one per month to one or two each week.

In every dream there are many people going about their daily life. I am in the scene but initially just as an observer. Then all of a sudden catastrophic events start occurring; everyone is panicking and screaming, and they want to know what is happening. I find that I am the one who is shouting out to everyone that what is happening is the fulfillment of Bible prophecy concerning the end-time signs of the approaching return of Jesus and the beginnings of the end of the world.

Each time the Lord empowers me to speak with His authority about these things in order to tell the people: should they not survive these events, if they do not know Jesus Christ as their Lord and Savior, they will end up in hell. I keep repeating the message over and over again, emphasizing that God's Word says that they will not enter the kingdom of heaven if they have not been born again (see John 3:1–8).

In these dreams I am informing the people as to what the Bible says must happen that will fulfill the signs of Jesus' soon return and about the rapture of true believers and about complacent, halfhearted believers being left behind on the earth after the rapture. I am also warning people about the tribulation period that will occur after the rapture and the rise of a new world order/one world authority of nations and "religious" organizations that will control the whole world (see Revelation 13:11–18; 17:1–18).

I would like to point out that I have not yet read the *Left Behind* fictional series of books by Tim LaHaye and Jerry B. Jenkins, and so I have not gained any of what I am about to write in this book from that influence. The Lord has given me specific words, and I have then sought Him about these things; and it seems that He is answering my questions with dreams and visions.

All I seem to do in these dreams is warn everyone about the end times. I am not given to see any fruit borne from speaking this message; I do not see anyone respond to it. The people just listen to it while they rush around in a terrified panic. It seems to me that all the Lord wants me to do is speak about what His Word says regarding the return of His Son, Jesus Christ, about the signs that will accompany it, and also about the end of the world.

Occasionally my dreams then switch to a vision of heaven with its beauty, peace, and glory and the amazing, iridescent, multicolored light that cascades all around everything that exists in heaven. But mainly the dreams are of the catastrophic end-time events that will come upon the earth at the appointed time, which only the Lord knows.

I kept asking the Lord what I was supposed to do with these dreams; surely there had to be a purpose as to why I was having them, seeing as they were increasing dramatically in their frequency. Then, on October 29, 2012, on the first anniversary of the date I picked up my pen to begin writing the manuscript of my first book, *Come on Church! Wake Up!*, the Holy Spirit revealed to me simply but powerfully that the reason for all these dreams was to warn believers and unbelievers that the return of Jesus Christ and the end of the world *is* coming, and to tell them what Jesus has to say about it. And so I felt I must obey the Lord in this, which is the reason I am writing this book. What is really incredible is that the moment I obeyed the Lord and began writing the manuscript for this book, the end-times dreams that the Lord was giving me so frequently completely stopped and I have not had another one since! This is a confirmation to me that He gave me those vivid dreams specifically to compel me to obey Him in writing this book.

A New Perspective

I feel that the Lord has caused the "veil to drop" or the "scales to fall" from my eyes. I now seem to observe life very differently from the way I used to. I look at everything in life from the eternal perspective.

While God's Word says He will not reveal when the end of the world will be, He *does* want His children to open their eyes, look around them, and discern if what they are seeing is a fulfillment of His Word in relation to end times. Jesus has told us that we need to be *so* observant that we will actually know when His return is "at the door" (see Matthew 24:32; Mark 13:29).

For the past three years, I have been simply observing things and searching the Scriptures about them. I have tried to verbalize what I am seeing to other believers, but have often been met with uninterested, blank expressions and a hasty change of subject. It has been hard for me to grasp the fact that many brothers and sisters in Christ do not seem to be interested or concerned in the slightest about the staggering, escalating, global evidence of end-time signs occurring on the earth, in the heavens, and in the sea.

I am left with the silent question inside me, asking, "Why do those who profess to be followers of Christ *not* want to believe that the end times that Jesus speaks about could actually occur in our current life time?" It would seem that many believers live their lives as if it will *never* occur.

As I have said before, there seems to be much discussion and debate about the end of the world, largely from a secular and non-biblical perspective, and it would also appear that there are more nonbelievers who are seeking information about the end of the world than there are actual believers. This is startling when we realize that the revelation of the end of the world was first given by the Lord to the Old Testament prophets who spoke these prophecies to the children of Israel.

These have been repeated throughout the centuries. During Jesus' earthly ministry, He graphically repeated the end-time warnings and signs to His followers. Then these are recalled in passages in the apostles' letters and epistles, and finally, they are again revealed by Jesus to the apostle John in the Book of Revelation. In view of this, how is it that so many believers today seem uninterested in talking about the subject of the end of the world? At best, it is often treated as if it is a fairy tale; but at times the subject is responded to with disdain.

Let me repeat—the end of the world is the fulfillment of the will of God. It is about the Second Coming of His Son, Jesus Christ, the end of this existing world, and the coming of the new heaven and the new earth. This ought to make believers excited and eager to be watchful for the signs of His approaching return and make themselves ready for that glorious day. At that appointed time, the Lord will return to redeem those who have put their faith and trust in Jesus as their Lord and Savior and are living their lives in obedience to His Word.

As believers, we ought to be diligent and vigilant in our watch for the signs of the return of our Bridegroom. We cannot claim to be ready for Jesus' return if we are failing to observe and discern what is happening in the world.

While many followers of Christ seem to be half asleep where this vital issue is concerned, it is staggering that so many unbelievers seem to be very interested in the subject of the end of the world yet will not accept that Jesus Christ has got anything to do with it.

As we will see later in this book, Jesus makes it clear in Scripture that those who do not believe in Him or who have rejected Him will not enter the kingdom of heaven when He returns and when the world finally comes to an end. God's holy Word makes it abundantly clear that their eternal end will be in the lake of fire (see Revelation 20:15). These are God's words, not mine.

So, to simply be interested in the subject of the end of the world, but *not* come to the conclusion that we need to confess our sins, repent of them, and turn to Jesus to save us from eternity in hell is *utter* futility. If one is not a believer, what is the point in being interested in the subject of the end of the world, when the fulfillment of it will catapult that soul into eternal hell?

I have heard it preached by Christian leaders that hell is *just* eternal separation from God. When I have heard such preaching with no further explanation from the preacher, I have felt the piercing sword of the Holy Spirit as it prompts me deep within to make a note that while what was preached was technically true, it was not the whole truth. Left as it is, it would deceive people into thinking that they will be okay being separated from God for eternity. Bear in mind that a huge percentage of the global population are quite content living their earthly lives without God anyway and would no doubt conclude that it is no big deal for them to live without God for eternity either.

For the church to reduce the horrific reality of spending eternity in hell down to a weak and powerless statement that hell is *just* eternal separation from God is to abandon the duty that God has placed upon the church, which is to bear witness not only to the Cross of Christ and the gospel message of salvation through faith in Jesus Christ, but also to the full reality of the horrors of eternal torment in hell for all who refuse to believe that Jesus came to save them from spending eternity in that horrific place.

The New Testament is packed with scriptures about the reality and horrors of hell. Most of these are spoken by Jesus Himself. How is it that some leaders in the church are comfortable with casually reducing the words of Jesus Christ to such a trivial and power-less statement? How will unbelievers, who are already unknow-ingly living their lives under the control of Satan, ever escape from the outcome of eternal torment in hell if the church fails to preach to them the realities of such an end as written down in the Word of God? These powerful scriptures are written in the Bible for us to preach so that unbelievers will wake up when they hear what awaits them if they remain an unbeliever.

The realities of the horrors of hell *also* need to be preached to believers to encourage them to remain obedient to God's Word, because the consequences of backsliding and remaining in that state are the same as the consequences for unbelievers, as the Scriptures will show throughout this book.

How the Lord must grieve when He hears His church water down the truth about the horrors of eternity in hell, when His love for all mankind compelled Him to send His Son, Jesus Christ, to die on the cross and shed His blood so that the way would be opened for all mankind (*if they will believe in Jesus*) to be saved from experiencing such devastating and catastrophic eternal consequences.

I also hear preachers say, "We don't want to frighten people into believing." Well, spending eternity in hell is something everyone ought to be frightened of, so it ought to be preached.

It seems that the church has watered the reality of hell down to a concept, saying, "It is just eternal separation from God, that's all." *That's all*? How can any Christian preacher say that that is *all* hell is? What a lie! The truth about hell is in the Holy Bible! If preachers won't preach the truth about it, we owe it to ourselves to search the Scriptures so that we will not allow ourselves to be misled and deceived by watered-down doctrine.

I believe that the teaching of many preachers is leading the sheep directly to the mouth of hell. Just because a preacher preaches something, it is not a guarantee that what was preached is the truth. It may be partially true or a complete lie. We will only know for certain if we diligently read and study the Word of God for ourselves. If we consume the Word of God as a matter of life and death, the Holy Spirit will prompt us when something that has been preached is only partly true or is completely false doctrine. Believers cannot afford to be continually spoon-fed all the time by preachers. No disrespect to our many diligent and trustworthy leaders, but it is possible that there are many leaders who could be feeding us spiritual "junk food" every week without us realizing it. The only way we will know for certain is when we start feeding from the Word of God for ourselves.

Many leaders and members of their congregations, while they may be believers, seem to be displaying large areas of unbelief in their lives and ministries. They display the evidence of double mindedness. Some parts of the Word of God they fully believe but many other parts they do not believe, and they resist the requirement to submit in obedience to the holiness of God's Word. They keep the parts of God's Word that seem easy and reasonable to believe, but they baulk at and discard the "tough stuff." They resist the hard things that His Word says to them; and so they dismiss them as irrelevant, out of date, and no longer necessary.

Even though God's Word has something to say about many areas in society that are causing friction, discord, and division in the present day; many leaders claim that the church must move and change with the times and accommodate, accept, and embrace the practices of the unbelieving culture we live in, despite the fact that our modern culture openly declares that it does not want anything to do with God.

Today's unbelieving culture obviously has the free will choice to reject anything to do with God. But the Christian church as a whole should not incorporate the "values" of an unbelieving society as part of its modern and "emerging" image in an attempt to attract them. "They call me the Most High, but they don't truly honor me" (Hosea 11:7b).

For the church to move and change with the modern times,

incorporating the values and secular beliefs of the unbelieving world is to openly declare that preaching the existing Word of God that has been proclaimed to the world from the very beginning of our existence is not adequate to do the job of saving, forgiving, cleansing, delivering, healing, and restoring the lost.

Jesus is the author of eternal salvation "*for all who obey him*" (Heb. 5:9, NIV, emphasis added), and the gospel message of salvation through faith in Jesus Christ is God's way of salvation.

Yes, the church is to receive into its midst all those who come, whatever state their life may be in. However, much of the church today restructures its doctrines and ministries to accommodate the existing practices of the unbelieving world in order to make it more comfortable for them to settle into the church.

How will those who are new to the church and new to the Christian faith ever be set free from the practices they are engaged in if the church feels it ought to respond to and comply with the demands of political correctness by tolerantly accepting and embracing these now legally deemed "acceptable" practices of the unbelieving world? The current cultural climate seems to be forcefully pushing the Christian church to "evolve" into something that unbelievers can come and dwell in without those unbelievers having to confess and repent of the practices that are part of their lifestyle of unbelief. The church is being swayed by the massive tide of cultural change and is being swept along with the "expectations" that the unbelieving world is demanding of it.

There seems to be an attitude towards the church from the unbelieving culture that says, "If you do not accept and do what we want, we will take whatever measures are necessary to make you comply." But rather than standing firm and remaining rooted in the Word of God, the church is caving in to the unrelenting pressure to conform, feeling that it has to find a way to evolve in order to survive and to appease the demands of a world culture that wants to be accepted by the church and be a part of it but *doesn't* want to obey God's Word.

In the Old Testament, when Solomon built the temple of God, it had to be built to the exact requirements that the Lord had laid down; and nothing evil, unholy, unclean, or impure was allowed to enter it. Under the New Testament when we become born again, our bodies are now declared to be the temple of the Holy Spirit; God considers them to be His temple. Therefore nothing evil, unholy, unclean, or impure should be permitted entry into our lives once we have become born again. Our bodies must no longer be used as "instruments of unrighteousness" (Rom. 6:13, KJV). If we continue in the sins we have previously been involved in when we were unbelievers, we are then deliberately defiling our bodies, allowing sin and all manner of evil practices to enter into and defile the temple of the Holy Spirit.

When the modern church accepts, embraces, and in some cases even "blesses" the unholy practices of some of its clergy and also some of the members of its congregation, the church is in a dire and very dangerous spiritual condition. The purpose of the church is to preach the gospel message of salvation (see Mark 16:15, NIV), baptize those who have confessed and repented of their sins (see Matthew 3:5–6; Acts 2:38, NIV), pray for them to receive the baptism of the Holy Spirit (see Acts 2:1–4, NIV), and then disciple them into living holy lives in accordance with the entirety of God's Word. The apostle Paul confirms this to Timothy,

> I solemnly urge you in the presence of God and Christ Jesus, who will someday judge the living and the dead when he appears to set up his Kingdom: Preach the word of God. Be prepared, whether the time is favorable or not. Patiently correct, rebuke, and encourage your people with good teaching. For a time is coming when people will no longer listen to sound and wholesome teaching. They will follow their own desires and will look for teachers who will tell them whatever their itching ears want to hear. They will reject the truth and chase after myths.
>
> —2 Timothy 4:1–4

Jesus warns us,

> Go back to what you heard and believed at first; hold to it
> firmly. Repent and turn to me again. If you don't wake up, I
> will come to you suddenly, as unexpected as a thief.
> —REVELATION 3:3

However, if disciples refuse to give up their sinful practices,
making excuses for what they are doing and have no regret,
remorse, or shame concerning their unrepentant sin, God's Word
says that they are to be put out of the church.

> I can hardly believe the report about the sexual immorality
> going on among you—something that even pagans don't do.
> I am told that a man in your church is living in sin with his
> stepmother. You are so proud of yourselves, but you should
> be mourning in sorrow and shame. And you should remove
> this man from your fellowship.
>
> Even though I am not with you in person, I am with you
> in the Spirit. And as though I were there, I have already
> passed judgment on this man in the name of the Lord Jesus.
> You must call a meeting of the church. I will be present with
> you in spirit, and so will the power of our Lord Jesus. Then
> you must throw this man out and hand him over to Satan so
> that his sinful nature will be destroyed and he himself will
> be saved on the day the Lord returns.
>
> Your boasting about this is terrible. Don't you realize that
> this sin is like a little yeast that spreads through the whole
> batch of dough? Get rid of the old "yeast" by removing this
> wicked person from among you. Then you will be like a fresh
> batch of dough made without yeast, which is what you really
> are. Christ, our Passover Lamb, has been sacrificed for us. So
> let us celebrate the festival, not with the old bread of wicked-
> ness and evil, but with the new bread of sincerity and truth.
>
> When I wrote to you before, I told you not to associate
> with people who indulge in sexual sin. But I wasn't talking

about unbelievers who indulge in sexual sin, or are greedy, or cheat people, or worship idols. You would have to leave this world to avoid people like that. I meant that you are not to associate with anyone who claims to be a believer yet indulges in sexual sin, or is greedy, or worships idols, or is abusive, or is a drunkard, or cheats people. Don't even eat with such people.

It isn't my responsibility to judge outsiders, but it certainly is your responsibility to judge those inside the church who are sinning. God will judge those on the outside; but as the Scriptures say, "You must remove the evil person from among you" [Deut. 17:7].

—1 CORINTHIANS 5:1–13

This is how seriously God views the situation, but how often does the church apply God's instruction to remove unrepentant believers from its congregations? God will not tolerate sin remaining in His temple, be it the corporate church or within the individual believer. When will the church and its members believe that God means what He says, and stop accepting and condoning all the practices of sin that it is lovingly embracing in the "spirit of tolerance"?

It seems that many in the church of this present time have lost sight of how horrendous sin is in the sight of God. It seems that the church is preaching that God is no longer concerned about sin because of His grace. What does the Word of God say about this?

What shall we say then? Shall we continue in sin, that grace may abound? God forbid. How shall we, that are dead to sin, live any longer therein?

—ROMANS 6:1–2, KJV

How do followers of Christ become holy? By believing in and obeying the Word of God on every matter of life and diligently putting into practice, without compromise, all that His holy Word instructs, exhorts, warns, and even commands us to do. Also by trusting in the power of the Holy Spirit to transform us and enable us to resist all the temptations that Satan will use to entice us to sin again and to keep on overcoming each onslaught that Satan hurls at us.

Followers of Christ are in a spiritual battle every second of their lives from the moment they become born-again to the moment they die. Satan wants to destroy those who are true believers and shipwreck their faith. His ultimate aim is to cause believers to forsake the Lord and reject their faith in Him, thereby causing their ultimate eternal end to be in the lake of fire along with Satan and his demons. We are greatly deceived if we think this is not the case.

In her book *Ready or Not—He is Coming*, UK author Stephanie Cottam writes,

> Is satan real? Is he really out to deceive the Church, to keep her away from her Beloved? Is he really trying to hinder you from being ready for the greatest wedding day you will ever attend? You'd better believe it! He is very definitely hard at work trying to deceive Jesus' Bride, with his army of fallen angels, every minute of every day! But sadly, many Christians do not believe it![1]

Further she says,

> The Bible describes satan as the god of this age, *2 Corinthians 4:4: whose minds the god of this age has blinded.* And it is clear, as the Light of Christ shines on it, how the domination of the god of this age is blinding the minds and hearts of men and women all over the world, to the truth of the Messiah. We see this in children's cartoons which are based on demonic-looking characters who "take over" the body/mind/spirit of the hero with "special" powers; music videos which are overtly sexualised or pagan-ritualistic; films and

television programmes which glorify violence, death, reincarnation and immorality, rather than life and love; society's acceptance of anything and everything which goes
against God's Word and against His laws, but a total rejection of God Himself. Things which were once seen as evil are
becoming celebrated, whilst those things which were once
deemed moral are now being ridiculed and frowned upon.

It is clear that the god of this age has an agenda. As we
draw closer to the return of the Bridegroom for His Bride,
we see it intensifying as it tries to distract the Bride from
keeping a look out for her Groom. You only have to switch
on the television for a few minutes to see how the media has
become a vessel for the agenda of the god of this age, and the
speed with which it is spreading and intensifying.[2]

The following scripture seems to reflect the culture of the times
we are now living in: "What sorrow for those who say that evil is
good, and good is evil" (Isa. 5:20).

Even the church has jumped on this worldly bandwagon by the
modern use of the word *wicked* to mean something that is good,
great, and fantastic. I have heard church leaders say things like,
"Wow, that camp last week was really wicked!" and "Wow, what a
wicked prayer meeting we had last night!" Come on, church! Wake
up! What are we doing twisting the meaning of the word *wicked*
to make it mean something that is good? Do we realize we are
fulfilling the scripture above? The church should not be involved
in twisting the Word of God. The Bible is cram packed with the
word *wicked*, and *never ever* does it transpose its meaning to be
something that is good. The biblical meaning of the word *wicked*
is something that is evil, sinful, and an abomination in the sight
of the Lord; and anything that is wicked will end up in the lake of
fire for eternity.

The culture of the present time is exerting immense pressure
on the church to agree with society's modern view that the things
that we have inherently known to be wicked and evil since the

time God created the whole world are now not wicked at all. In fact the church is being coerced into "reassessing" what the holy Word of God clearly states is wicked and evil. This tsunami of coercion is causing the church to actually question whether God's Word is correct.

There seems to be an unspoken question permeating throughout the church, effectively saying, "Perhaps God's Word is wrong after all. Perhaps what He says isn't the truth. Perhaps we need to reinterpret His Word in the light of the culture we are living in."

Since the time the Word of God was established, the church has known that what His Word says is for our own protection and ultimately for our good. But the unrelenting pressure of the world is asking the church to overturn God's Word on what is good and what is evil. In effect it is saying, "We don't want to know about what God states is for our own good. What sort of a good God would tell me that I should not pursue a lifestyle that 'pleases me'? What's God's opinion got to do with anything? It's my life and my body, so I will do whatever I please. I don't need God's Word to tell me what's good for me, and what is evil."

It would seem that the same people who make these sorts of statements are the very ones who want and expect the church to allow them to dwell in the church and to affirm and bless them in their lifestyle choices, when in fact the church should be preaching and teaching the need for confession, repentance, and renouncement of these practices.

The church is crumbling under the pressure to accommodate wickedness in its midst. It is God's Word that declares what is evil, whether the world likes it or not. The world's opinion about it doesn't change the fact that God's Word declares such things to be wicked. Only the lies and deception of Satan would cause the situation where the church begins to question the truth and authority of God's Word, which has stood the test of time for thousands of years since the time it was first established. God's

Word and His truth are eternally unchangeable and will stand forever (see Isaiah 40:8).

God is *not* going to rewrite His holy Word just to please the will of man. Man seems quite proud of himself when he rewrites the Word of God into a version that suits and pleases what he wants, but doing this does *not* make God's established Word obsolete.

God's Word will stand forever, despite the multitudes of reinterpreted and rewritten versions that man takes upon himself to create to fit his choices. If the church continues to question and suppress the plain and simple truth of God's Word and carries on with its acceptance and blessing of sin within God's holy temple, God's Word says that His wrath will fall upon all who are engaged in such wickedness.

> The wrath of God is being revealed from heaven against all the godlessness and wickedness of people, who suppress the truth by their wickedness, since what may be known about God is plain to them, because God has made it plain to them.
> —Romans 1:18–19, niv

Satan's ultimate aim is to deceive followers of Christ and cause them to abandon their faith. If Satan is successful in this goal, those who were once part of the bride of Christ will find that they have lost their salvation and their ultimate end will be in the lake of fire, along with Satan and his demons. This is Satan's agenda. Do not let him deceive you any longer... *wake up!*

It is no good trying to pretend that hell does not exist. Some leaders even preach its nonexistence and then package it as new and up-to-date "Christian" doctrine. It is *not* new doctrine! It is false doctrine packaged up to look like Christian doctrine. True Christian doctrine tells us that hell *does* exist because Jesus has said it does.

So when we preach that hell does not exist, we are declaring Jesus to be a liar. Who do we think we are to preach doctrine to both the believer and the unbeliever that is diametrically opposed to the words of Jesus Christ? Have we no conscience that would cause us to tremble in fear of His holy and just judgment? Have we no shame that our preaching of such false doctrine is leading multitudes of people to believe our lies that will ultimately end in their eternal torment in the hell that we refuse to preach about?

Just because we may personally not believe that hell exists, our unbelief does not mean that it does not exist. Jesus says that it does exist, and so what Jesus has to say about it is the truth and the final say on the matter. If we carry on in our unbelief of hell's existence, we will one day find ourselves experiencing the horrendous eternal torment of the hell we refused to believe existed. At that point it will be too late to cry out to God to save us and forgive us for not believing what He has said. Our fate will be eternal; we will only have ourselves to blame.

Oh the folly of mankind to continually crave after and believe manmade doctrine that comforts what its "itching ears want to hear" (2 Tim. 4:4), and condones what the lust of its flesh wants to satisfy.

The Lord God says, through the prophet Jeremiah,

> When people fall down, don't they get up again? When they discover they're on the wrong road, don't they turn back? Then why do these people stay on their self-destructive paths? Why do the people...refuse to turn back? They cling tightly to their lies and will not turn around. I listen to their conversations and don't hear a word of truth. Is anyone sorry for doing wrong? Does anyone say, "What a terrible thing I have done?" No! All are running down the path of sin as swiftly as a horse galloping into battle!
> —JEREMIAH 8:4–6

And again the Lord says,

> How can you say, "We are wise because we have the word
> of the LORD," when your teachers have twisted it by writing
> lies? These wise teachers will fall into the trap of their own
> foolishness, for they have rejected the word of the Lord. Are
> they so wise after all?
>
> —JEREMIAH 8:8–9

How dare we erase the parts of the holy Word of God that we
do not agree with and insert our own doctrine in its place and
then call our manmade doctrine the Word of God! Have we for-
gotten that God is righteous, holy, and just and is able to take away
our names from the Lamb's Book of Life? (See Revelation 22:19.)

Will we never come to our senses and wake ourselves up from
the deadly slumber of deception that we have fallen into, which
will destroy us if we remain under the control of the evil one who
is creating this slumber of deception?

The fires of hell are burning, and we are mindlessly heading in
its direction because we prefer to believe man's false doctrine that
hell doesn't really exist instead of believing the holy Word of God
which states clearly and unambiguously that it *does* exist; and it
will exist for eternity, and all who do not believe it exists will end
up being tormented in it for eternity.

But even though the servants of the Lord shout out these warnings to the world, still the world will not listen; still it will not
respond. Regardless of this fact, these warnings must still be
preached!

The Lord God says through the prophet Jeremiah,

> But my people would not listen to me. They kept doing what-
> ever they wanted, following the stubborn desires of their evil
> hearts. They went backward instead of forward....But my
> people have not listened to me or even tried to hear....Tell
> them all this, but do not expect them to listen. Shout out
> your warnings, but do not expect them to respond.
>
> —JEREMIAH 7:24, 26A, 27

Concerning unbelievers, many of them may wish the world would come to an end as soon as possible, falsely believing that it will at last bring to an end all the burdens, pressures, hardships, pain, and suffering of their daily lives on this earth. It is true that when Jesus returns and the world as we know it comes to an end, all pain and suffering will cease; but as Scripture tells us, this will *only* be for those who have confessed and repented of their sins, have put their faith in Jesus Christ as their Lord and Savior, and who are living their lives on earth in readiness for His return. The end of all pain and suffering is the eternal reward for those who will be permitted to enter the kingdom of heaven.

There is much false doctrine being preached that deceives people into believing that everyone will enter the kingdom of heaven, regardless of whom or what they believe or don't believe. This "doctrine" makes a mockery of Christ's crucifixion on the cross. As we will see in scripture throughout this book, this teaching is *not* the teaching of Jesus Christ. It is the teaching of those who the Bible says are a false christ, a false messiah—they are workers for the prince of darkness, known in the Bible as the antichrist, the devil, and Satan.

Concerning the false doctrine of Universalism, which teaches that everyone will go to heaven whether they have faith in Jesus Christ or not, J.C. Ryle, who lived from 1816–1900 and whose ministry in the Anglican Church spanned fifty-eight years, wrote in his book *Are You Ready for the End of Time? Understanding Future Events from Prophetic Passages of the Bible*:

> In the day of Christ's Second Advent...hope, the plank to which they now cling, and on which they generally depend to the very last, hope will be entirely taken away in that awful day. They will seek salvation with earnest, but not be able to find it. They will run hither and thither in a vain search for the oil of grace. They will knock loudly at the door of mercy, and will get no answer. They will cry, "Lord, Lord, open to

us," but all to no purpose. They will discover to their sorrow that opportunities once let slip can never be regained, and that the notion of universal mercy always to be obtained, is a mere delusion of the devil. Who does not know that thousands are urged to pray and repent now, who never attempt it? They mean to try some day perhaps.... They fancy it will never be too late to seek the Lord. But there is a time coming when prayer shall be heard no longer, and repentance shall be unavailing.[3]

Further, he says,

There is much about hell in Revelation. There are many fearful expressions, which show its reality, its misery, its eternity, its certainty. How deeply important it is to have clear views on this solemn subject in this present day! A disposition appears in some quarters to shrink from asserting the eternity of punishment. A flood of that miserable heresy, universalism, seems coming upon us.... Tender-hearted women and intellectual men are catching at the theory that, after all, there is hope in the far distance for everybody, and that Satan's old assertion deserves credit, "Ye shall not surely die." Oh, reader, beware of this delusion![4]

Even though Ryle wrote these words in the nineteenth century, how well they apply to our current times. And how right that he uses the word *theory* in relation to the doctrine of Universalism.

There are also those who do not believe in God but believe that when their mortal flesh dies, that's the end of life. They don't believe that they have a soul that will rise from their body and will live for eternity in heaven or in hell.

Again, there are many who believe that when they die their soul will come back to life in some other form; and when that form then dies, their soul moves on again into another life form in a never ending cycle of life, supposedly for the soul to learn something that they may have failed to fully learn in their "previous lives."

All of this is contrary to holy Scripture. Physical death will come to us all, and the Word of God says that "we will all stand before the judgment seat of Christ" (Rom. 14:10b) and will have to give account of what we have done with our lives on earth (see v. 12).

> None of us can hold back our spirit from departing. None of us has the power to prevent the day of our death. There is no escaping that obligation, that dark battle. And in the face of death, wickedness will not come to the rescue of the wicked.
> —ECCLESIASTES 8:8

None of us will escape that "divine appointment," that day of reckoning. But what will our eternal outcome be?

The end of the world reality for the unbeliever will be vastly different from the blessings that are reserved solely for the true believer. This is covered in chapters 6 and 7, but I would encourage you not to skip straight to those chapters because all the preceding chapters are vital to the whole picture.

So, the purpose of this book is to focus predominantly on the biblical revelation of the end of the world and what Jesus has to say about it. The end of the world is solely about Jesus' Second Coming; and, as such, Jesus' word on the subject is the *only* authority and the only word that matters. All other versions and opinions of the end of the world that are not grounded in the truth of the Word of God are therefore based on falsehood and will lead many into a false sense of peace that "all will be well" for them when the end of the world comes or if they die before it ends. God's Word does *not* say that "all will be well" for everyone when the end comes.

With this in mind, let's begin our journey into what Jesus has to say about what appears to be one of the hottest topics of conversation in the world today.

Chapter 2
WHAT JESUS SAID: THE GOSPELS

That day of judgment will come, says the Sovereign LORD.
Everything will happen just as I have declared it.
—EZEKIEL 39:8

IN THE GOSPELS Jesus has a great deal to say about events that will indicate the approaching end of the world. The church would do well to heed His warnings, and wake up out of its slumber. Before we look at scriptures from the Gospels on this subject, let's open our eyes and see what is going on in the world around us in these present times, because what is coming upon the earth in our time is hardly insignificant and definitely not irrelevant.

I realize that by the time this book is published and is in the hands of the reader, a lot more will have happened upon the earth than what I am writing at the beginning of this chapter. But at the time I started handwriting the draft manuscript at the end of October 2012, the East Coast of America was facing a storm of catastrophic proportions—Hurricane Sandy—which was described as the worst storm in living memory. Only the day before, the West Coast was on high alert for a tsunami following an earthquake in the North Pacific Ocean.

While isolated weather events have occurred throughout history, we now seem to be living in a period of time where all these events seem to be happening extremely close together on an unprecedented and ever increasing scale, even on a daily basis. Over the past three years I have observed this with silent shock. Each day produces yet another disaster or catastrophe of some sort:

- Hurricanes, tornadoes, violent and destructive hail-storms with hailstones the size of golf balls (or bigger)

- Extreme flooding, earthquakes, and earth tremors in places around the world, which don't normally experience such events. Many of these now occur so frequently that the inhabitants of those places have barely recovered from the previous incidents.

- Tsunamis, lightning storms, volcanic eruptions, landslides, extreme snowstorms, famines, and droughts occurring in places that normally produce an abundance

- Disease and pestilence (epidemic and pandemic); mysterious and sudden deaths of masses of fish, dol-phins, seals, turtles, and whales which are being washed up on the shores and floating in rotting heaps in rivers and oceans

- Birds mysteriously and suddenly dying, dropping out of the sky in huge numbers onto the streets, in fields, and in people's gardens; other animals such as cattle suddenly dying all at the same time. All of these mysterious deaths are happening with no "rea-sonable" explanation.

- Enormous forest fires devastating hundreds of square miles of land and property; mysterious dis-eases affecting up to one-third of the tree population in some countries, and which appear to be spreading around the world

- Strange and often eerie-looking unnatural cloud formations, which suddenly appear "out of nowhere" and bring with them bizarre and extreme weather conditions which were not expected

- Escalating wars between nations, increasing civil wars and civil unrest, rumors of potential impending wars; terrorist threats and acts of mass destruction and genocide; violence, suicide bombings, riots, increasing rebellion against law and order in previously peaceful places, and a rising tide of general lawlessness around the world

- Increasing global economic and social collapse; financial, political, and religious corruption and scandal; and increasing immoral and sexual scandal throughout society, including within political and religious organizations

This is a long list; but this is only the tip of the iceberg, merely the visible signs, while much more destruction could be underneath the surface waiting to explode onto the face of the earth.

To anyone who does not know Jesus Christ as their Lord and Savior, these events must be causing great anxiety, fear, and dread at what will happen next. I have noticed the increase in the number of reported suicides, as people find themselves in such distress that they are unable to cope with life anymore and so decide to "end it all."

But to someone who believes in Jesus Christ, these ever increasing signs should cause us to search the Scriptures for evidence and answers and ultimately reassurance from God's Word.

While I was reading through the Gospels for the scriptures relating to the end-time events, I noticed that they were all contained in the Gospels of Matthew, Mark, and Luke. I have been a Christian for twenty-one years, but this fact had never even occurred to me. So, I asked the Lord why the apostle John had not recorded in his Gospel, Jesus' words about the end times. Immediately the Lord spoke straight to my heart saying, "Because I personally showed him a revelation of what will happen at the end, which he recorded in the Book of Revelation."

It is amazing when the Lord reveals something to us that afterwards seems so obvious that it staggers us that we were oblivious to it. This is how I know with certainty that the Lord heard my question and answered it directly, because it had never dawned on me in twenty-one years.

So let's begin our search in the Gospels and see what Jesus has to say about the end of the world and what will be the signs of the end times. The following are the Gospel scripture verses from the New International Version, which I am using to make up a complete picture of what Jesus says will be the signs of the end times.

- Matthew 24:3–44

- Mark 13:5–37

- Luke 21:8–36

- Matthew 25:31–46

Many of the verses are almost identical in each of the Gospels, so I have pieced the events that Jesus has listed in the order that He has spoken them from each Gospel, without repeating the identical verses. This is so that the full picture becomes clear. We will see that Jesus is not rattling off a list of end-time events in some haphazard manner. He is listing each event as it unfolds onto the earth, and then He tells us what will follow after each event until the end of the world comes.

It is extremely detailed and warns believers that we must be on our guard, be alert and keeping watch for all these events as they happen, and be aware of what will come next in the sequence of events. We really cannot afford to continue living as if these things couldn't possibly happen in our lifetime.

Why can't they?

From what we see happening all around the world today, escalating more and more as the days and months go by, the end-time signs that Jesus warns believers about may actually be underway. We should not ignore or dismiss this possibility.

Note, as we will see in the scripture passages below, Jesus says that no man will know the day or the hour of His return; but Jesus Himself has warned us that we *must* keep watch concerning the signs of the end times in order to know when His return is "at the door."

Stephanie Cottam says, "Ours is *not* to know the day or the hour, our place is just to make sure we are ready and not sleeping, and that those around us are also ready and not sleeping."[1]

Are we living our lives in this watchful manner? Are we as leaders preaching this to the flock, or are we afraid that, if we do, our congregations will think we have become fanatical and jumped onto the secular world's end-time bandwagon? (This is very different from the biblical end-time truth.) As a church, as leaders, and as individual believers, we cannot continue to ignore the truth and the reality that has been spoken to all believers out of the mouth of our Savior Jesus Christ.

Below is my compilation of Matthew 24:3–44, Mark 13:5–37, and Luke 21:8–36, which I have combined and reworded somewhat using primarily the New International Version to give one overall text of what Jesus says will be the signs of the end of the world:

> Later, Jesus sat on the Mount of Olives. His disciples came to Him privately and said, "Tell us, when will all this happen? What sign will signal your return and the end of the world?" Jesus answered: "Watch out that no one deceives you. For many will come in my name, claiming, 'I am the Christ' and

'the time has come," and will deceive many. Do not follow them.

"You will hear of wars and rumors of wars, and revolutions, but see to it that you are not alarmed; such things must happen, but the end is still to come. Nation will rise against nation, and kingdom against kingdom. There will be famines, earthquakes and pestilence in various places, and fearful events and great signs from heaven. All these are the beginnings of birth pains. You must be on your guard. Before all this, they will lay hands on you, and you will be handed over to the local councils and be flogged in the synagogue and be persecuted and put to death.

"On account of Me you will stand before governors and kings as witnesses to them. And the gospel must be first preached to all nations. When you are arrested and brought to trial, do not worry beforehand about what you will say. Just say whatever is given to you at the time, for it is not you speaking, but the Holy Spirit, for I will give you the words and wisdom that none of your adversaries will be able to resist or contradict. At the time many will turn away from the faith and will betray and hate each other, and many false prophets will appear and deceive many people. Because of the increase in wickedness, the love of most will grow cold. Children will rebel against their parents and have them put to death. Brother will betray brother to death, and a father his child. You will be betrayed, even by your own parents, relatives and friends. All men will hate you because of Me, but he who stands firm to the end will be saved. Not a hair of your head will perish. And the gospel of the kingdom will be preached in the whole world as a testimony to all the nations, and then the end will come.

"When you see Jerusalem being surrounded by armies, you will know that its desolation is near. So when you see standing in the holy place 'the abomination that causes desolation' spoken of through the prophet Daniel—let the reader understand—then let those who are in Judea flee to the mountains, let those in the city get out, and let those in the country not enter the city. Let no one on the roof of his house go down or enter the house to take anything out. Let no one in the field go back to get his cloak. For this is the time of punishment in the fulfillment of all that has been written. How dreadful it will be in those days for pregnant women and nursing mothers! Pray that this will not take place in winter or on the Sabbath, because those will be days of distress unequaled from the beginning, when God created the world, until now—and never equaled again. There will be great distress in the land and wrath against this people. They will fall by the sword and will be taken as prisoners to all the nations. Jerusalem will be trampled on by the Gentiles until the times of the Gentiles are fulfilled. If those days had not been cut short, no one would survive, but for the sake of the elect whom He has chosen, those days will be shortened.

"At that time if anyone says to you, 'Look, here is the Christ!' or 'There he is!' do not believe it. For false christs and false prophets will appear and perform signs and miracles to deceive even the elect—if that were possible. So be on your guard; I have told you everything ahead of time. So if anyone tells you, 'There he is, out in the desert,' do not go out; or 'Here he is, in the inner rooms,' do not believe it. For as lightning that comes from the east is visible even in the west, so will be the coming of the Son of Man. Wherever there is a carcass, the vultures will gather.

"But in those days following that distress the sun will be darkened, and the moon will not give its light; the stars will fall from the sky, and the heavenly bodies will be shaken. There will be signs in the sun, moon and stars. On the earth, nations will be in anguish and perplexity at the roaring and tossing of the sea. Men will faint from terror, and apprehension of what is coming on the world, for the heavenly bodies will be shaken.

"At that time they will see the sign of the Son of Man appear in the sky, and all nations on earth will mourn. They will see the Son of Man coming on the clouds of the sky, with power and great glory. And He will send His angels with a loud trumpet call, and will gather His elect from the four winds, from the ends of the earth to the ends of the heavens.

"When these things begin to take place, stand up and lift up your heads, because your redemption is drawing near. Now learn this lesson from the fig tree, and all the trees; as soon as its twigs get tender and its leaves come out, you know that summer is near. Even so, when you see all these things happening, you will know that the kingdom of God is near, right at the door. I tell you the truth, this generation [the generation that sees these things begin to happen] will certainly not pass away until all these things have happened. Heaven and earth will pass away, but my words will never pass away.

"No one knows the day or the hour, not even the angels in heaven, nor the Son, but only the Father. As it was in the days of Noah, so will it be at the coming of the Son of Man. For in the days before the flood, people were eating and drinking, marrying and giving in marriage, up to the day Noah entered the ark; and they knew nothing about what would happen until the flood came and took them all away. Two men will be in the field; one will be taken and the other left. Two women will be grinding with a hand mill; one will be taken and the other left. Be on guard! Be alert! You do not know when that time will come. It is like a man going away: He leaves his house and puts his servants in charge, each with his assigned task, and tells the one at the door to keep watch. Therefore keep watch because you do not know when the owner of the house will come back—whether in the evening, or at midnight, or when the rooster crows, or at dawn. If he comes suddenly, do not let him find you sleeping. What I say to you, I say to everyone: Watch! Understand this: if the owner of the house had known what time the thief was coming, he would have kept watch and not have let his house be broken into. So you must also be ready, because the Son of Man will come at an hour when you do not expect him.

Be careful, or your hearts will be weighed down with dissipation, drunkenness and the anxieties of life, and that day will close on you unexpectedly like a trap, for it will come upon all those who live on the face of the whole earth. Be always on the watch, and pray that you may be able to escape all that is about to happen, and that you may be able to stand before the Son of Man."

—AUTHOR'S COMPILATION OF
MATTHEW 24:3–44, MARK 13:5–37, AND LUKE 21:8–36

When the Son of Man comes in his glory, and all the angels with him, he will sit on his throne in heavenly glory. All nations will be gathered before him, and he will separate the people from one another as a shepherd separates the sheep from the goats. He will put the sheep on his right and the goats on his left. Then the King will say to those on his right, "Come, you who are blessed by my Father; take your inheritance, the kingdom prepared for you since the creation of the world. For I was hungry and you gave me something to eat, I was thirsty and you gave me something to drink, I was a stranger and you invited me in, I needed clothes and you clothed me, I was sick and you looked after me, I was in prison and you came to visit me." Then the righteous will answer him, "Lord, when did we see you hungry and feed you, and thirsty and give you something to drink? When did we see you a stranger and invite you in, or needing clothes and clothe you? When did we see you sick or in prison and visit you?" The King will reply, "I tell you the truth, whatever you did for one of the least of these brothers of mine, you did for me." Then he will say to those on his left, "Depart from me, you who are cursed, and into eternal fire prepared for the devil and his angels. For I was hungry and you gave me nothing to eat, I was thirsty and you gave me nothing to drink, I was a stranger and you did not invite me in, I needed clothes and you did not clothe me, I was sick and in prison and you did not look after me." They also will answer, "Lord, when did we see you hungry and thirsty, or a stranger or needing clothing or sick or in prison, and did not help you?" He will reply, "I tell you the truth, whatever you did not do for one of the least of these, you did not do for me." Then they will go away to eternal punishment, but the righteous to eternal life.

—MATTHEW 25:31–46, NIV

What an incredible long and vivid account this is from Jesus about the things that will happen as the end of the world approaches! It is something we cannot ignore, but it would seem that much of the church today is operating in denial of what Jesus is saying in the texts above. The church appears to be like the servant who, instead of remaining vigilant on his watch for his master's return, began to live his life in a complacent manner associating himself more with the things of the world. We must be wary of falling into this trap.

In Mark 13:35–37, Jesus, speaking to His disciples, is very insistent that not only they, but also all believers, remain vigilant on their watch for His return. "What I say to you, I say to everyone: 'Watch!'" (v. 37, NIV).

Let's now examine the long text in detail. Remember that Jesus is giving these warnings to His *disciples* to be watchful for the signs and ready for His return, *not* to unbelievers. People who are not followers of Jesus do not feel any necessity to be watchful and ready for His return.

Firstly, Jesus warns that false christs will come to deceive believers and that we are not to follow them. A thorough online search will reveal the rise in false messiahs over the last few years!

Then He says that we will hear of wars, rumors of wars, and revolutions, but we are not to be alarmed at the news of them. Famines, earthquakes, pestilence, and other fearful events and great signs from heaven will also occur, which "are the beginning of birth pains" (Matt. 24:8, NIV). The mainstream news of recent years has gradually got to the point of being inundated with evidence of all these events taking place on a daily basis. So have the birth pains Jesus refers to already begun?

Jesus says before all this happens believers will be handed over to those in positions of authority and will be flogged, persecuted, and put to death. Evidence that this is happening more and more is reported on our daily news, and I recently heard that more Christians have been martyred in the last one hundred years than in all the preceding centuries since Jesus was crucified! If this is the case, then in the past one hundred years, Jesus' words concerning believers being persecuted and put to death is being fulfilled. So, what follows are an increase in wars, rumors of wars, famines, earthquakes, pestilence, and other fearful events and great signs from heaven, etc. We are witnessing an escalation in all these events.

Jesus informs us that we may have to be a witness for Him to governors and kings, and that the gospel must be preached to all nations. With the use of computer technology, it is now possible to preach the gospel to the ends of the earth at the touch of a few buttons. We can reach government leaders, kings and queens, and other high ranking officials quickly and easily through computer technology. We no longer have to stand on our "soap box" in the streets in order to preach the Word of God.

Then Jesus says that a time will come when many believers will turn away from faith in Him and begin to betray each other. This would seem to be a time when many false prophets will arise and deceive many into believing their "different gospel" (see Galatians 1:6–9). As there is going to be a great falling away from the true gospel, those who have abandoned the faith will be easy pickings for the false prophets to deceive. I believe this has been happening throughout history, but is now occurring today on a large scale.

Jesus says that wickedness will increase and that it will cause people to lose their love for others. The New Living Translation describes it as, "Sin will be rampant everywhere" (Matt. 24:12). It is as though people are so shocked by the increase in wickedness that is happening around them and around the world that they no longer want to show love or care to others because they can't trust anyone anymore. Many of us don't even know who our neighbors are, let alone have any care for any needs they may have. Also many people, particularly in the UK, are now so suspicious of others that they display warning stickers on their front doors to the effect that they will not open the door to anyone who knocks without a previously arranged appointment.

Wickedness has certainly been increasing quite significantly in society in the past few years, and this has had a knock-on effect in how people treat one another. When our love for others grows cold, we develop a "couldn't care less" attitude to almost everything and everyone. When an increasingly large number of people begin to display this attitude in our local communities, towns, cities, nations, and indeed globally, we can expect fear and trembling to occur on an unprecedented scale. Lawlessness will sweep across the nations of the world like an unstoppable tsunami leaving catastrophic devastation in its wake.

Jesus says that children will rebel against their parents and have them put to death. There has been an escalation in the last few years of children rebelling in very big ways, causing huge destruction to neighborhoods, property, and businesses. I have not yet heard of children putting their parents to death for their faith in Jesus Christ, but as Jesus commands, "Watch!" for it will happen.

Furthermore, Jesus warns us that believers will be betrayed by their own parents, relatives, and friends and that all men will hate us because of our faith in Him. But He also tells us we must stand firm in our faith until the very end so that we will receive our salvation. There is increasing evidence around the world of believers being hated by all men because of their faith in Jesus, and I am sure we have all been on the receiving end of other family members and friends who no longer want to talk to us or associate with us because of what we believe.

Jesus says that when all the nations of the world have been reached with the gospel, then the end will come. We could actually do an Internet search to find out how far the gospel has spread into the world and if there are any nations left that have not yet heard the gospel. If all the nations of the world have had the gospel preached to them and there are believers in all the nations who are trying to spread the Word of God, then we need to be extremely alert and watchful for the approaching end.

Jesus says that one of the signs of the imminent end will be that Jerusalem will be surrounded by armies (countries wishing to destroy Israel) and that its desolation is near. An abominable figure that causes the desolation of Jerusalem will stand in the holy place to bring about Jerusalem's desolation. The holy place referred to is the temple of God, which has not existed since its destruction in AD 70. Therefore, to fulfill this end-time prophecy, the temple must be rebuilt. (See recommended reading: *The New Temple and the Second Coming* by Grant R. Jeffrey.) When people see these things happening they are to flee for their lives and not go back to their houses to get anything. It will be a catastrophic time of great distress, the likes of which the world has never seen. Jerusalem will be trampled and crushed by Gentile nations for a period of time, but the Lord will cut these days short.

My husband recently did a search of the current nations that are hostile to Israel, and he put colored stickers on a large map to see just how many of them surrounded the nation of Israel. We were horrified at what we saw! As it stands, Israel is currently surrounded by many nations that are opposed to it. Clearly, as each day goes by, the fulfillment of Jesus' words concerning the desolation of Jerusalem are drawing ever closer. But looking at the map of the increasing number of countries that are hostile to Israel, could this fulfillment even be imminent?

Jesus says that people will again say that He has returned, but says we are not to believe what they say; because when He finally returns, His appearing will be visible from the east to the west. We will not have to have somebody point it out to us. His return will be visible to all mankind.

> Look! He comes with the clouds of heaven. And everyone will see him—even those who pierced him. And all the nations of the world will mourn for him. Yes! Amen!
>
> —REVELATION 1:7

Jesus says that in the days that follow the distress in Jerusalem, the sun will become dark, the moon will not shine, the stars will fall from the sky, and the heavenly bodies will be shaken. The heavenly bodies are the sun, the moon, the stars and the planets, which includes the earth. God will make these all begin to shake. (See Isaiah 2:19; 13:13; Joel 3:16; Haggai 2:6–7, 21, NIV.)

When something is being shaken, it moves. We will visibly see and feel the effects of this shaking, and it will cause people's hearts to fail them in terror as they are suddenly faced with the fact that the world is disintegrating and there is nothing anyone can do about it. It has been prophesied by the Lord that the world will come to an end; and as such it will be fulfilled, no matter how much environmental conservation work is undertaken by the human race in an effort to reverse what is escalating upon the earth.

Individual online research will reveal reports that the moon seems to have rotated about 30 degrees so that the face of the "man in the moon" that we normally see has now slipped downwards. If it isn't the moon that has rotated, then it would appear that something has happened to the earth, causing it to shift off its original axis. If it is the earth that has moved in some way, then any shift would cause a distortion in the earth's magnetosphere, which could lead to freak and violent weather conditions all around the globe.

Further individual research will also reveal reports about strange things happening with the sunrise and the sunset. I have personally witnessed for myself some unusual occurrences with the sun, when I heard the Lord instruct me to "look up" and see. The back of our house faces directly north, and on several occasions during the height of the summer of 2012, the sun set severely northwest, in fact in the north to northwest segment. I called my husband to witness it, and also contacted my sister to observe it and to confirm that I was not imagining it. The following day it set exactly west, then the day after that it set northwest, then back to north/northwest, swinging about like a pendulum on a daily and weekly basis.

I have researched moonrise dates and the corresponding shapes of the moon for a given month and then observed the moon shape and compared the visible evidence with what the official data says it should be. I have been shocked at how different it is on many occasions. A few times the shape of the moon was two days ahead of the shape it should have been. I am aware that I am not the only person to have observed these signs in the heavenly bodies. If Jesus says that there will be signs in the sun, moon, and stars, then we have to look up and witness these things. This is something we should be actively watching out for instead of being distracted and overly absorbed by our daily routine and the cares of life. God has given us eyes to see; and He exhorts us to be watchful and observe signs in the sun, moon, and stars, as these will be indicators that we are in the end times.

Jesus says that great anguish will come upon the nations as they witness the great roaring and tossing of the sea. This could indicate massive tidal shifts such as tsunamis and other great flooding from the sea caused by bizarre abnormal weather patterns, such as occurred in the UK in December 2013–January 2014.

Jesus also says that mankind will faint with terror because of what is coming upon the earth. There is much increasing evidence already of people being terrified at what is already happening upon the earth. We witness daily the overwhelming terror that grown men are now facing as their lands are destroyed, their businesses ruined, and their livelihood stripped away from them in an instant due to catastrophic weather conditions or disease that decimates the livestock and crops of the farming industry year after year. Many people are being made redundant due to global economic issues, with no hope of another job as they join the endless queue with others who have also been catapulted into the same position. Many commit suicide, as they see no point in living anymore. All they have ever worked for is gone, in one moment. They can no longer pay their bills, their homes are repossessed or they are evicted, and they have no money to buy food to feed their families. All of a sudden their comfortable, peaceful, and secure lifestyle is destroyed beyond recognition due to devastating and catastrophic events and also political, social, and economic decisions made by global powers that they have never even heard of.

If what the earth is currently experiencing is actually the beginning of birth pains, it is beyond our imagination to be able to comprehend what the suffering and devastation will be like as the final end unfolds. When birth pains begin there is no stopping the final delivery. Jesus says that when men's hearts fail them with terror at what is happening on the earth, *then* the sign of His appearing will be seen in the sky. He will come in the clouds with great power and glory, sending His angels with a loud trumpet call.

He will gather His faithful ones (the believers who have remained alert and watchful and lived their lives in readiness for His return) from all the corners of the earth and the heavens. This event will be the long awaited rapture. Jesus says that when we see His return in the sky, we are to stand up and lift up our heads because our redemption is about to happen.

As I have mentioned before, Jesus says that we must be so watchful of the signs of the times that we will actually know when His return is at the door. He says that no one will know the day or the hour of His return, although there has been much false prophecy concerning predicted dates for His return. We can be sure that those who do this are false prophets whom Jesus has told us to ignore. So anyone who predicts specific dates for the Rapture is a false prophet, a liar, and sent out by Satan to deceive and cause believers to fall away in the last days from the true gospel of Jesus Christ.

Over the years I am sure we have all heard of various names and religious organizations which have predicted and proclaimed dates for Jesus' return. When that date has arrived and Jesus has not returned, they just dismiss it as a simple miscalculation, without any explanation for their errors, and then they set a new predicted date. An Internet search will reveal that in 1843 William Miller predicted that Jesus would return sometime between 1843 and 1844; in 1876 Charles Taze Russell, founder of the Jehovah's Witnesses, predicted the great day of the Lord would be in 1914. Since then the society has predicted many other dates for Jesus' return, all of which have failed. Most recently Harold Camping predicted the end of the world to be on May 21, 2011, and when that failed he amended it to October 21, 2011. There are many others who have made predictions through the centuries.

Some false prophets have deceived their followers, teaching them that they must commit suicide if Jesus fails to return on their predicted date. Again, an Internet search reveals that in 1978 Jim Jones claimed to be a reincarnation of Jesus and ordered his 900 followers to commit suicide by drinking a concoction containing cyanide; in 1993 David Koresh also claimed he was God, and he and eighty of his followers burned to death in the siege that took place in Waco, Texas; in 1997 Marshall Applewhite, another self-proclaimed Messiah and the leader of the Heaven's Gate sect, organized for his thirty-eight followers to commit suicide. This kind of situation surely has to be religious deception at its worst. People currently claiming to be the reincarnation of Jesus are Sung

Myung Moon, the leader of the Unification church, and Jose Luis de Jesus Miranda, a pastor in Miami who claims he is God.

The world is seeing the fulfillment of Jesus' warnings of the rise in false messiahs and false prophets. Do not listen to the lies of these people who deceive you with doctrine that contradicts God's holy Word, or you will become ensnared in false doctrine and false religion with disastrous eternal consequences. God's Word makes it very clear that *no one* will know the day or the hour of Jesus' return (see Matthew 25:13). Our part is to keep watch for the biblical signs of the approaching end and to warn each other to make ourselves ready for that Day. We are *not* to exalt ourselves to a position of prophesying dates for Jesus return when the Bible states clearly that no man, no angel, and not even Jesus will know the time of His return, *only the Father* (see Matt. 24:36).

When we claim to predict the date of Jesus' return, we are actually claiming to know information that only God knows. This type of activity is the deceiving work of Satan, and it is leading millions of people to follow the puffed up declarations of these false prophets. There is only one place such predictions will lead to—eternity in hell for all who continue to believe the lies of these false prophets whom Satan is using upon the earth. Heed God's warnings and flee from such teaching!

Jesus continues with His teaching about the signs of the end times, saying that right up to His return people will just be carrying on with their lives with complete disregard and disinterest that the world is about to end, just like they did at the time of Noah, when God wiped mankind from the face of the earth in the great flood (except for Noah and his family).

Jesus says that at the Rapture many will be left behind. He warns us that if we don't want to get left behind, we must be on guard, alert, and watchful and not be careless by letting our hearts be weighed down with drunkenness and the anxieties of life. It is sad to say that many believers are living their lives as if Jesus will never return. They are caught up more in the things of this world such as excessive involvement with leisure pursuits, entertainment, and socializing. God is not concerned when we engage in these activities in moderation in order to participate in Christian fellowship with one another. But when they become dominant in our lives and use up the time that we know we should be giving in devotion and worship to God, that is where things become a problem, causing us to take our focus off the urgent need to be living in an alert, diligent, and watchful manner for all that Jesus is warning us about concerning the end times.

If we fall into that trap, the day of Jesus' return will come upon us suddenly and unexpectedly when we are not ready for Him. He says that if we want to escape all that is about to happen on the earth after the Rapture (i.e., the tribulation period—see the next chapter of this book), we must be watchful so that we may be able to stand before the Son of Man on that glorious day of our redemption.

Pastor Seung Woo Byun, in his book *Christians Going to Hell*, writes,

> When Jesus returns, He will come as a bridegroom. Jesus will come to take His bride. Therefore, we must be ready as His bride. Then what is the most important preparation for His bride? That is having true love for her bridegroom. This occurred to me during one dawn prayer meeting. I was reading Luke 17:32–35 with the saints:
>
> "Remember Lot's wife! Whoever tries to keep his life will lose it, and whoever loses his life will preserve it. I tell you, on that night two people will be in one bed; one will be taken and the other left. Two women will be grinding grain together, one will be taken and the other left."
>
> Suddenly, the Holy Spirit came powerfully upon me. He spoke clearly to my spirit: "Do you know why when the Lord returns, two people will be in one bed but one will be taken and the other left? It is because one loved the Lord while

living his Christian life, while the other did not love the Lord while living his Christian life. As the Scripture is written, 'Look, the bridegroom!' Jesus will come as a bridegroom and will take away His bride. Therefore, only those who love the Lord sincerely will be lifted up.[2]

When I personally came to this same passage of scripture during my study of the Gospels in order to work on this chapter, I felt the Holy Spirit clearly say to my spirit that this passage related to believers and that as many as 50 percent of those who believe they are Christians will be left behind. That is precisely what Jesus indicates in Matthew 24:40–41. The Lord revealed this to me a couple of months before I had even purchased Pastor Seung Woo Byun's book.

I am certain that a huge majority in the church today believe that this passage is saying that all believers will be taken and that it is the unbelievers who will be left behind. I believe this thinking is incorrect. Jesus was speaking to His disciples at that time. And immediately after He spoke the words about one being taken and the other left behind, He said, "So you, too, must keep watch! For you don't know what day *your* Lord is coming" (Matt. 24:42, emphasis added).

The fact that Jesus uses the words *"your Lord"* makes it clear that this verse is an instruction from Jesus to *believers* to keep watch or they may find themselves left behind. Jesus would not be instructing *unbelievers* to "keep watch" because they have not made Him their Lord and they don't even believe that He is the Messiah who is going to return. Unbelievers are not concerned about spending eternity in heaven with Jesus, so in their own minds they would have no need to keep watch for His return.

Jesus says that at His return, all nations will stand before Him and He will separate the people from one another as a shepherd separates the sheep from the goats. The sheep are the faithful and true believers who have obeyed His Word and done what He asked them to do. They will hear the words, "Come, you who are blessed by my Father; take your inheritance, the kingdom prepared for you since the creation of the world" (Matthew 25:34, NIV). The goats are the people who did not obey the Lord or do what He asked; and they will hear the words, "Depart from me, you who are cursed, into eternal fire prepared for the devil and his angels" (v. 41, NIV).

With all my heart and soul, I want to be counted among those who will hear those beautiful and precious words, "Well done, my good and faithful servant" (v. 21); and, "Come, you who are blessed by my Father; take your inheritance, the kingdom prepared for you from the creation of the world" (v. 34, NIV). Don't you want to hear these words spoken to you, too? Jesus has told us what we need to do, so let's get about doing it. Time may be short, and we do not want to be caught out unprepared at His appearing or we may find ourselves separated from the other sheep and heading for eternal doom and torment with the goats.

On the subject of being ready for the return of the bridegroom, Stephanie Cottam writes,

> The days we are living in are the last days. These days are crucial, and we have limited time to get ready! Just as a bride will do all she can to get ready for her wedding day, we have to do all we can to make ourselves ready for Jesus' return! And just as a bride has very limited time to get ready on the day of her wedding, our time is now very limited.[3]

If we profess to follow Christ, our lives must display the good fruit of righteous and holy living, in obedience to His Word. So much is at stake when we live out a complacent and compromising version of Christianity, kidding ourselves that because we say we are a believer we will be okay and will make it through when Jesus returns. Jesus solemnly warns us of the seriousness of this:

> If anyone hears my words but does not keep them, I do not judge that person. For I did not come to judge the world, but to save the world. There is a judge for the one who rejects me and does not accept my words; *the very words I have spoken will condemn them at the last day.*
> —JOHN 12:47–48, NIV, EMPHASIS ADDED

Jesus is saying here that the purpose of His first coming was not to judge the world but to open up the way of salvation to all mankind. But if we reject his Word and do not obey it, on the last day it is *His Word* that will judge us and it will also condemn us. Our rejection and disobedience will bring us into the place of judgment by the authority of His Word.

When this happens, the Lord will *not* rejoice in the eternal judgment that must come upon all those who reject His Word. It will grieve Him immensely, as He does not want anyone to perish in eternal hell but all to come to repentance (see 2 Peter 3:9). But in the end His Word will be the final judge, and it is our rejection of His Word and our unrepentant rebellion and disobedience of it that will bring us face-to-face with the final verdict of His Word. This is an immensely serious matter, one that we dismiss lightly at great eternal peril.

The Bible uses the term "children of disobedience" (Eph. 2:2, KJV; 5:6, KJV; Col. 3:6, KJV). So who are the children of disobedience? Having taken time to reflect upon this before the Lord, I believe that the children of disobedience are disobedient Christians who refuse to give up their sinful practices and remain unrepentant. Allow me to explain why I believe this.

If we take unbelievers as an example, they do not believe in God or His Word, and so they are under the influence and the power of the god of this age, who is Satan. Unbelievers only accept and follow the practices of the world. Their master is Satan (whether they realize this or not), so they do what the worldly influences entice them to do. Without realizing it, unbelievers blindly obey the desires and wishes of Satan, which is evident in the cultural climate of this present day. They do not believe in God and His Word and so they have no "obligation" to obey it, as God is not their Master. Unknowingly they have made Satan their master, because of their choice *not* to believe in God and His Son, Jesus Christ. As God is not their Master and they are not obliged to obey His Word, this is why I believe that unbelievers are not the children of disobedience.

However, if we are believers our Master is God and we are subject to His Word and His commands. If, as a believer, we rebel against His Word, I believe that this makes us the "children of disobedience." We can only really disobey someone whom we have accepted as being in authority over our lives. If a person is a believer, God is in authority over them and so they become "children of disobedience" when they rebel against His Word.

Unbelievers have not accepted God as having authority over their lives, and as such, His Word has no place in their life. They have rejected God and His Word and they are not bound to live by what His Word says. This is why I conclude that unrepentant believers are the "children of disobedience," as this term cannot apply to unbelievers who have not made God their Master to obey. So if unbelievers are not the children of disobedience in the eyes of the Almighty God, what sort of children are they?

> The one who does what is sinful is of the devil, because the devil has been sinning from the beginning. The reason the Son of God appeared was to destroy the devil's work. No one who is born of God will continue to sin, because God's seed remains in them; they cannot go on sinning, because they have been born of God. *This is how we know who the children of God are and who the children of the devil are.*
>
> —1 JOHN 3:8–10A, NIV, EMPHASIS ADDED

Therefore, my conclusion from the Word of God is that disobedient and unrepentant Christians are the children of disobedience. The unbelievers who have chosen not to believe in God or His Word are children of the devil.

So, if we are believers and are not living in obedience to His Word, we will be judged by His Word accordingly and will receive what is due to us as written in His Word (see Revelation 20:11–13). God is serious about what He says. We resist, reject, and disobey His Word at our peril.

Chapter 3
WHAT JESUS SAID: THE
BOOK OF REVELATION

This is a revelation from Jesus Christ, which God gave
him to show his servants the events that must soon take
place. He sent an angel to present this revelation to his ser-
vant John, who faithfully reported everything he saw. This
is his report of the word of God and the testimony of Jesus
Christ. God blesses the one who reads the words of this
prophecy to the church, and he blesses all who listen to
its message and obey what it says, for the time is near.

—REVELATION 1:1–3

L ET'S READ THAT passage again and let its power and authority
sink in. God gave the revelation to His Son, Jesus Christ, so
that Jesus could show us, His servants, what *must* soon take
place. God revealed it to Jesus; then Jesus revealed it to the apostle
John who faithfully reported everything he saw. The passage states
that this (all that is written in the Book of Revelation) is his report
of the Word of God and the testimony of Jesus Christ.

This is an astounding passage of scripture with an amazing
statement of its faithfulness. If we profess to be a follower of the
Bridegroom, we had better believe this revelation that Jesus is
showing us and treat the entirety of what we are about to discover
with reverential fear and awe of the holiness and justice of God.

The Book of Revelation is such a vital book on the end-time
events, given by Jesus to the apostle John, that I would love to
write out the whole text from chapters 4 to 22, but this would take

up almost half of this book. Even as I begin this, I am certain this will be the longest chapter that I write.

I will do my best to condense the information in a running story, but by no means does this imply that I am removing anything from the Book of Revelation (see Revelation 22:19). I simply want to highlight what Jesus is saying will happen at each event and then write my own thoughts on it which I will offer as suggestions, indications, and possible representations.

However, what I write I will do so humbly before God with a prayerful heart, trusting in His guidance to lead me and His mercy and grace to forgive me if I am in error. I do not wish to offer my thoughts as fact; they are merely my thoughts, although I have taken much time in prayer about them. Each reader is free to study and research the things I offer or to reject them.

I encourage you to read the full Bible text for yourself in a version of the Bible that you find easy to understand, such as the New Living Translation, which is the version I am using to write the text into a running story.

Chapters 4–22 are the written account of the revelation of the end of the world given by Jesus Christ to the apostle John. It is full of detail, much of it very graphic. In chapters 1–3 Jesus gives many warnings to His church to basically wake up and repent of their ongoing sinful behavior and attitudes and get their Christian lives and their churches cleaned up in readiness for His return. I will not cover those chapters here, as I wrote on this in my first book, *Come on Church! Wake Up!*, which I would strongly like to encourage you to read.

I will start where the vision given to John begins, in chapter 4. It would be good to note that the revelation of the end of the world is given *immediately after* Jesus' letters of warning to the churches to repent of the sins that they are allowing to remain in their own lives and in their churches as a whole.

The vision of the end of the world is not all a bed of roses for those who claim to be believers, which, I am sure, is why Jesus' letters of warning to the churches *precede* the actual vision. It is as if Jesus is saying, "Look, church! I am about to reveal to you what will happen to many of you who call me 'Lord! Lord!' but do not do the things that I say. Heed My warnings in My letters to you so that I do not have to shut the door on you for failing to make yourselves ready for My return."

The revelation Jesus gives to John is a graphic vision of the catastrophic, cataclysmic collapse of the whole world prior to the final end. As we will see, at a certain point God begins the unveiling of revelation. It begins with the opening of the seven seals.

When an important document is bound with a wax seal, the importance of the contents of the document that is sealed remains hidden until a specific, appointed time. At that appointed time when the seal is opened, the contents of the document are made known to all that the sealed document pertains. The seal is opened, the contents are revealed, and they cannot be reversed.

Once the first seal of the Book of Revelation has been opened, from that moment on the world is on the *final* countdown towards Jesus' Second Coming. As the events of a seal are fulfilled upon the earth, each successive seal is opened in turn and the whole world will experience the devastating and catastrophic consequences that each seal reveals.

At the beginning of this book, I shared with you the overview phrases that the Lord has given to me regarding the last few years. For the year 2010, the words were "the unveiling of revelation." At the time I did not know exactly what that meant, but very quickly I felt that a turning point had been reached in the spiritual realm. I felt a deep sense that the Lord was saying "the time has come" for the events of the Book of Revelation to unfold; and so I started to keep my eyes and ears open for end-time signs on the earth, in the heavens, and in the seas, which is what Jesus has exhorted us to do in the Gospels.

Up to that specific point on December 31, 2009, I had no thought or belief that the end of the world could possibly occur in our life-time and so I had no focus on signs of the end times at all.

But in that instant, the words the Lord gave me catapulted my thinking into a new dimension. All of a sudden I felt God was saying to me, "Open your eyes and look! What I have said in My Word is about to begin. I am about to unveil the events that I have spoken of in the Book of Revelation in fulfillment of My entire prophetic Word concerning the end of the world."

I have to admit that I was very daunted and burdened with this message, and have not known what to do with it for the past three years, until I felt the Lord give me the title of this book, *The End of the World, and What Jesus Has to Say About It.* I then knew with a deep conviction that the Lord was leading me to write all the words He has given me for each year in this book.

From the time He gave me the words "the unveiling of revelation," I have begun to see things very differently. And as I have said previously, when I have tried to share them with other believers, I am frequently met with silent, blank stares. I am shocked that the vast majority of believers are not really interested in the subject of the end of the world, let alone being asked to even consider the possibility that it could occur in our generation. It's as if they have got "better" things to think and talk about.

Well, the end of the world has to occur at some point, so why do we seem to dismiss it as something that is millennia away? The return of Jesus and the end of the world could occur tomorrow if God decides that it should. God is the *only* One who knows when that time will be, but Scripture exhorts us to be of the mindset that it could be today, tomorrow, or *any* day. We must not live as if it will never happen in our lifetime. We should live every day as if it *will* happen in our lifetime. That way we will *always* live in read-iness for Jesus' return. But it seems the bride of Christ hardly gives the return of her Bridegroom a second thought, and we allow our minds and our lives to be distracted and occupied with anything and everything else.

Let's be honest with ourselves. Let's seriously examine our lives. How much time each day, each week, and each month do we spend thinking about Jesus' return and the end of the world? If we are truly honest, many of us will say we struggle to even think about what was preached in the Sunday sermon. Satan's tactic is to distract us and cause us to take our minds off the most important part of the reason why Jesus is coming back—to take home with Him all believers *who are obedient and ready* at His appearing, and to usher in the end of the world as recorded in the Book of Revelation.

Those believers who are not obedient to His Word and are not ready will be left behind at His appearing to experience the horrors of the tribulation, as we shall clearly see in God's Word. But many "unready" believers may not survive His return and will die at that point, and will have no further opportunity to repent, and they will then have to await the judgment. Stephanie Cottam writes,

> Too many of us are playing at Church. Too many of us are busy doing life. Too many of us will not be ready when the Lord returns to fight satan once and for all. Too many of us are in danger of being left behind.[1]

As believers, we cannot afford *not* to be ready when Jesus returns. Do we want to be left behind to experience all that we are about to discover in the Book of Revelation? If not, then I urge you to wake up—now! If "your actions do not meet the requirements of God" (Rev. 3:2), do something about it, *now!* Fall on your knees and confess your ongoing sins and repent of them, recommit your life to God and start living your life in obedience to His precious holy Word.

So, with all this in mind, let's have a look at what Jesus has to say about the end of the world in the Book of Revelation. After the apostle John had written down all Jesus' letters of warning to repent that were to be delivered to the churches, John is taken into the vision concerning the end of the world, with exact detail as to the order of events as the revelation unveiled before him.

I have included the scripture references so that you can read it in your own Bible and underneath each scripture reference is a summary I have made. Please do not rely solely on my summary. I ask that you would read it in conjunction with the full text in your own Bible.

REVELATION 4: HEAVEN

Summary

John sees a door standing open in heaven and is told that he must be shown what will soon take place. He then sees the throne of God in all its glory and the One who sits on it. He also sees the twenty-four elders dressed in white with gold crowns on their heads and sitting on thrones around the throne of God. He sees and hears lightning, rumblings, and thunder coming from the throne of God. There are four creatures around the throne; they are covered with eyes and have six wings and they praise the Lord day and night. As they do so, the twenty-four elders fall down to worship and praise the Lord and lay their crowns before the throne.

REVELATION 5: THE LAMB AND THE SCROLL

Summary

John then sees a scroll in God's right hand, sealed with seven seals. A mighty angel speaks loudly, asking, "Who is worthy to break the seals and open the scroll?" (v. 2, NIV). No one in heaven, on the earth, or under the earth could open it and John weeps. But then he is told that the Lion of Judah has triumphed and is able to open the scroll. A Lamb appears, standing in the center of the throne and it looks as if it has been slain. The Lamb takes the scroll and the twenty-four elders fall down before the Lamb. The elders hold golden bowls full of incense, which are the prayers of the saints (all the prayers of every true believer). The elders worship the Lamb, saying that He is worthy to open the seals of the scroll because He was slain and shed His blood to redeem people for God from every tribe, language, and nation. Then John sees and hears the voice of thousands upon thousands of angels around the throne, worshiping the Lamb that was slain. Then every creature in heaven, on the earth, under the earth, on the sea, and in the sea joins in singing worship to the Lamb. The four creatures around the throne say "Amen" and the elders fall down in worship.

Revelation 6:
The Opening of the First Six Seals

The following is what we will begin to experience upon the earth once Jesus has broken the first seal, and after that, all successive seals are broken. These are the things we need to be awake and alert to and not casually dismiss.

The first seal, summary

John sees the Lamb open the first seal, and a rider appears on a white horse wearing a crown and carrying a bow in his hand. He rides out as a conqueror determined on conquest.

Because this rider is on a white horse and wears a crown, many believe this rider is Jesus. But this cannot be the case as the events this rider brings about take place *prior* to the time when Jesus comes to rapture the true believers. The event where Jesus appears riding on a white horse relates to the final end of the world and does not occur until *after* the rapture; we see this recorded in Revelation 19:11–16.

To me, the rider of the first seal would appear to represent an earthly kingdom, as indicated by the crown and that he is bent on "riding" across the world in a defiant manner conquering other kingdoms and nations. The bow indicates a kingdom that has unrelenting war in mind and will not stop until it has completed its conquering.

There are kingdoms in existence and others rising up at this very time with unrelenting war on their minds, bent on destruction, and steadily pushing their way into territories and nations, overthrowing them, and establishing their rule over these lands.

The second seal, summary

John sees the Lamb open the second seal and sees a fiery red horse with a rider. This rider is given a large sword, and he is given power to take peace from the earth and causes people to kill each other.

To me, this would indicate a time of global unrest, distress, insecurity, and uncertainty. One moment peace is agreed and the next moment this "peace" is destroyed due to people killing each other through civil wars and nations warring against other nations for whatever reason. See Jesus' words in the Gospels. The large sword could represent the large-scale killing that will occur. This is happening around the world on an ever increasing scale.

The third seal, summary

John sees the Lamb open the third seal and sees another rider, this time on a black horse. The rider holds a pair of scales in his hand and John hears a voice saying there would be a quart of wheat for a day's wages and three quarts of barley for a day's wages and not to damage the oil and the wine.

To me, this would indicate a time after the events of the first two seals where the world will be so unstable due to unrelenting war and futile peace treaties that global economies will collapse causing prices to rise so high that it will cost people a day's wages for a loaf of bread—not just in a few underdeveloped countries but globally, including all the superpower nations. See Jesus' words in the Gospels about famines. These things are happening now and are on the increase.

The fourth seal, summary

John sees the Lamb open the fourth seal and sees a pale horse with another rider. The rider's name is Death. Hades (hell) follows close behind him. *They* (that is Hades and the rider called Death) are given power over a quarter of the earth to kill with the sword, with famine, with the plague, and by wild beasts.

To me, this would indicate a time that will come after the events of the third seal, where people will die from starvation, plagues, and being attacked and killed by wild animals, probably because the animals are also starving due to the worldwide famines. Killing by the sword could mean that people are killing each other because they are fighting over what little food there is available as well as being killed by the sword in war.

In the passage it mentions that Hades (hell) follows close behind all this death. This could indicate that many who die during the period of this devastating fourth seal may end up in hell.

All of the above things are happening on the earth right now. For example, there is an increase in people being attacked and killed by wild beasts where animals seem to be entering residential areas in search of food because their natural habitat is suffering from drought or from adverse weather-induced conditions.

The fifth seal, summary

John sees the Lamb open the fifth seal and sees under the altar the souls of all those who have been martyred because of the word of God and the testimony they have maintained. These souls cry out in a loud voice asking the Lord how much longer it will be before He brings judgment upon the world in order to avenge their blood that has been shed for maintaining their faith even unto death. John sees each of them being given a white robe, and they are told to wait a little longer until the number of fellow servants who are yet to be martyred is completed.

To me, this would indicate a time following all the terrifying events of the fourth seal where many who say they are a follower of Jesus Christ will be killed for their faith. This is already happening to Christians who live in many countries that are opposed to the Christian faith.

Before we look at what will happen when the Lamb opens the sixth seal, let's list the events of the first five seals in order.

1. A global power/kingdom will ride roughshod over the nations of the earth, bent on overthrowing and conquering every nation in its path.

2. This will bring about the end of peace of any kind and this conquering kingdom will cause people to kill each other.

3. This will cause global unrest, instability, and economic collapse so that global prices rise, resulting in famines and starvation because people can't afford to buy food.

4. This in turn will bring about death through starvation, the outbreak of plagues, and people being killed by the sword and by wild beasts across a quarter of the world.

5. Many who try to speak about Jesus will be killed.

Since hearing the words "the unveiling of revelation" for the year 2010, I have been stunned into a silence of reverential fear and trembling at what I have been witnessing just on our mainstream news. First it was some "breaking news" perhaps once a week, and then a few times each week. But now, in 2014, we are in a time where dramatic "breaking news" is covered from morning to night, with more and more added to it interrupting the main breaking news with more breaking news. Everything that is reported seems overwhelmingly catastrophic and utterly devastating.

One would think that all of the first five seals were already open. Perhaps they are? The opening of the seals is something that will happen in the heavenly realms, and then the events contained in each seal will begin to be manifested upon the earth. The problem would seem to be that believers may be expecting to actually see the four riders on their different colored horses galloping across the sky. And because they haven't witnessed this yet, they reject the possibility that the seals might actually already be open.

I am sure that some people will think I am deluded in what I have just said. That is okay; this is par for the course when writing about a subject that much of the church seems to prefer to ignore and doesn't wish to look at. It takes courage to really want to see and understand something that baffles us. I am certain that I am not deluded about this vital and urgent matter. Jesus has told us to keep watch for the signs of the times in order to know when "his return is very near, right at the door" (Matt. 24:33). I would suggest that those who are under a delusion about this would be believers who are not keeping watch as Jesus commanded. This delusion comes from Satan who wants as many believers as possible to be unwatchful and unready for Jesus' return.

The words the Lord gave me in sequence are:

- 2010—The Unveiling of Revelation

- 2011—Death and Destruction

- 2012—Cataclysmic Collapse

- 2013—Escalation

I have kept watch and seen that these words are being fulfilled as the Lord said. We must remind ourselves that once the first seal is open, it cannot be reversed, and all the events of all the subsequent seals will follow, as prophesied. They will continue on an escalating basis until the end comes.

So, whether the first five seals are already open or not, what does the sixth seal hold in store for us?

The sixth seal, summary

John sees the Lamb open the sixth seal. There is a great earthquake and the sun turns black, the moon turns blood red, and the stars fall to the earth. The sky is rolled up like a scroll and every mountain and island is removed from its place. Every king, prince, and general along with the rich, the mighty, and every slave and free person hides themselves in caves and among the rocks. They all cry out for the mountains and rocks to fall on them, to hide them "from the face of the one who sits on the throne and from the wrath of the Lamb" (v. 16) because this is the great day of the wrath of God and the Lamb upon the face of the earth. Who could survive it?

I think we would all agree that this great day of the wrath of God and the Lamb has not yet occurred upon the face of the earth. But to me it would seem that at a certain point during the events of the fifth seal (the killing of true believers), God will have had enough and things will occur that will be cataclysmic. When this "great day" occurs, it will cause everyone who does not obey the Word—from the least to the greatest—to flee for their lives. They will be desperate to be buried under rocks and in caves to be hidden from the wrath of God and the Lamb because of their rebellion and refusal to repent of their sins.

REVELATION 7: THE SEALING OF GOD'S PEOPLE AND THE GREAT MULTITUDE

Having covered the events of the first six seals, let's now look at what will happen as this "great day" unfolds.

Verses 1–8, summary

John sees four angels at the four corners of the earth and they are holding back the four winds to prevent them from blowing on the land, sea, and trees. Another angel appears from the east carrying the seal of God, and shouts to the four angels not to harm the land, sea, and trees until a seal has been put on the foreheads of the servants of God. John sees that the number of those who were sealed with the seal of God totaled 144,000; equal numbers from the twelve tribes of Israel.

Amongst the church today there is much speculation about who the 144,000 are or will be. There are organizations who claim to be counted within this number, which, to be honest, I would consider to be rather a self-exalting thing to do. If we were to add together all those who consider that they will be amongst the 144,000, I think we would find that the number would far exceed 144,000. So clearly there must be some criteria that determines who will be amongst the 144,000 who have the seal of God put on their foreheads. I will come to the criteria shortly.

Firstly, the passage says that 12,000 will come from each of the twelve tribes of Israel. Many suggest that this is purely symbolic, but I am of the mindset that believes that God means what He says, as He "is not the author of confusion' (1 Cor. 14:33, KJV). So if we do become confused over scripture, then there is only one being who has caused us to be confused—and it is *not* God. It is Satan, as he does cause confusion and turmoil in our minds by getting us to listen to the deception he sows in our thoughts. Satan absolutely loves it when he can get Christians to rip each other to shreds over the Word of God. He sows confusion and causes division because we will not simply accept and believe that God means what He says.

Allow me to digress from the subject of Revelation 7 for a few moments as I wish to say more about the division created by our often unwillingness to accept and believe that God means what He says. Jesus says we are to receive the kingdom of God like a little child (see Luke 18:16–17). This includes believing His Word. Little children are hardly going to intellectualize God's Word and spend hours, days, weeks, months, and years trying to interpret what it "really" means. Little children take what is said to them literally. This is what Jesus means when He says that we must receive the Word of God as little children.

In that case, as adults, why don't we just believe what God says and resist the need to interpret, intellectualize, and over spiritualize what He is clearly saying? Without the infilling of the Holy Spirit, man's natural, human interpretation of the Word of God causes a wrong understanding and wrong interpretation of His Word. The Bible says that without the Spirit, natural man cannot know the things of the Spirit (see 1 Corinthians 2:14); and since the Word of God is "Spirit and life" (see John 6:63, NIV), natural man cannot possibly understand His Word. All he is able to do is make up his own understanding and interpretation of it, which, without the Holy Spirit, will be gravely in error.

It is sad to say that many people who have never been filled with the Holy Spirit are preaching and teaching in our churches. This ought to cause us great alarm; because when a person preaches the Word of God but is not filled with the Holy Spirit, his own natural interpretation of Scripture will cause what he teaches to be false doctrine, no matter how good his intentions are. This can result in divisions occurring, which leads to the rise of "new" denominations of the church.

A town or city could have quite a large variety of denominations, all preaching something slightly different from each other. Many of these denominations may be reluctant or even unwilling to get involved with each other, not even to meet for corporate prayer for the salvation of the people of their communities. This is a desperately sad state for the global church to be in. The Lord sees all this, and I believe that the corporate church needs to repent of the sins that are causing each denomination to exist in isolation of its fellow churches. How can we expect God to bring local, national, and even global revival when we, as a church, are reluctant to meet with believers in other denominations of the Christian church to pray for such revival?

Each denomination, despite its differences from the other churches, is part of the whole body of Christ; yet for most of the time we are all acting independently of the other "parts" of the body. So we end up with all these parts of the body of Christ struggling to get along in the community and wondering why so few in our community seem to be interested in finding out about God or coming to church.

The result of the division and disunity of the churches would seem to be that the people in our towns and cities see all these denominations like severed body parts scattered about their community, all struggling with a measure of mistrust or even dislike for one another, for whatever reason, refusing to come together in the unity of Christ for the sake of the work of the Lord on this earth.

This evident division turns the lost even further away, as they are unsure about which church to even approach in order to find the truth. In the end many are so disillusioned, they instead settle on making up their own "faith" from the pick and mix varieties of godless belief systems that are widely available throughout the world.

All this may happen because many in leadership in the Christian church today are not Spirit-filled and do not want to receive and believe the Word of God like a little child, but prefer to assert their own understanding and interpretation of it into their preaching and teaching. The result of this is confusion both inside the church and also in the wider community, resulting in the church being seen to "adjust" its biblical belief and its doctrine to bring it in line with man's "modern interpretation." This can only end in total chaos for the body of Christ.

Now let's return to the subject of Revelation 7:1–8. If we believe and accept that the 144,000 will be made up of 12,000 from each of the twelve tribes of Israel, what are the criteria that make them so special that God has counted them worthy to be sealed with the seal of God before the four angels release the four winds to bring damage to the land, sea, and trees?

God has already made it clear who they are in His Word. We find this a bit further on in Revelation 14:1–5, but I will put parts of that passage below for clarity.

> Then I saw the Lamb standing on Mount Zion, and with Him were 144,000 who had his Name and his Father's name written on their foreheads....They have kept themselves as pure as virgins, following the Lamb wherever He goes. They have been purchased from among the people on the earth as a special offering to God and the Lamb. They have told no lies; they are without blame.
>
> —Revelation 14:1, 4–5

Notice this passage says, "They have kept themselves as pure as virgins....They have been purchased from among the people on the earth as a special offering to God and the Lamb. They have told no lies; they are without blame." So, in a nutshell, the 144,000 are servants of God from the twelve tribes of Israel who have not defiled themselves sexually, are as pure as virgins, have never lied, and are blameless.

If we are among those who claim that we are going to be part of the 144,000, we need to seriously examine ourselves. How dare any of us make this holy decision that we are worthy to select ourselves for what only God will select. Remember the story of James and John when they asked Jesus to let them sit at His right hand and His left hand in the kingdom of heaven? What was Jesus' reply?

> Then James and John, the sons of Zebedee, came over and spoke to him. "Teacher," they said, "we want you to do us a favor." "What is your request?" he asked. They replied, "When you sit on your glorious throne, we want to sit in

places of honor next to you, one on your right and the other on your left." But Jesus said to them, "You don't know what you are asking! Are you able to drink from the bitter cup of suffering I am about to drink? Are you able to be baptized with the baptism of suffering I must be baptized with?" "Oh yes," they replied, "we are able!" Then Jesus told them, "You will indeed drink from my bitter cup and be baptized with my baptism of suffering. But I have no right to say who will sit on my right or my left. God has prepared those places for the ones he has chosen."

—MARK 10:35–40

So, having examined ourselves and discovered that we don't meet the criteria for being one of the 144,000, many of us may feel crushed and believe there is no hope of entering the kingdom of heaven.

Do not despair! Read on!

Verses 9–17, summary

John then sees "a vast crowd, too great to count, from every nation and tribe and people and language" (v. 9). They are clothed in white and hold palm branches in their hands. They are standing in front of the throne of God and before the Lamb. They cry out praises to God and to the Lamb. All the angels are standing around the throne, the twenty-four elders, and the four living creatures, and they fall down before the throne with their faces to the ground and worship God.

One of the elders reveals to John that the great multitude of people clothed in white are those who have come out of the tribulation and have washed their robes in the blood of the Lamb and made them white. They will stand in front of the throne of God and serve Him day and night in His temple. They will never again be hungry or thirsty, the sun will not scorch them, Jesus will be their Shepherd and will lead them to springs of life-giving water, and God will wipe away every tear from their eyes.

Wow! What an awesome chapter! To me, this would seem to indicate the rapture of the multitude of the true believers who have kept watch and made themselves ready for the return of the Bridegroom. (I appreciate and accept that many in the church may have different views on this.) They have overcome to the very end by the blood of the Lamb. They have "come out of the Tribulation" could possibly be in the same way that God delivered Lot "out of" Sodom and Gomorrah *before* He brought His wrath and destruction upon it—indicating that God will deliver His Bride "out of" the Tribulation *before* He commences the wrath of the tribulation period. It seems that the rapture takes place just prior to the commencement of the events of the tribulation period, signaled by the moment when the Lamb opens the seventh seal.

Revelation 8:1–5: The Seventh Seal

Verse 1, summary

John sees the Lamb open the seventh seal, and there was silence in heaven for about half an hour.

Before I continue with this summary, I would like to say something about this verse. Heaven is a place of endless worship to God by all the host of heaven—the angels, the elders, the four living creatures, and anything else that exists in heaven. Can you imagine just how serious and catastrophic something would have to be to cause the whole of heaven to fall into utter silence for even one second, let alone half an hour?

Whatever the Lamb is about to unveil with the breaking of the seventh seal, all of heaven ceases its worship of God for half an hour, as they wait in complete silence for the event to unfold. The knowledge of this ought to make us shudder in reverential fear of what is about to come upon the earth.

Verses 2–5, summary

John sees the seven angels of God standing before Him and they are given seven trumpets. He sees another angel with a gold incense burner who stands at the altar. This angel is given a great amount of incense to mix with the prayers of God's holy people as an offering on the gold altar. The smoke of the incense mixed with the prayers of God's holy people rises up to God. This angel then fills the incense burner with fire from the altar and throws it down upon the earth. There is thunder, lightning, and a great earthquake.

REVELATION 8:6–13: THE FIRST FOUR TRUMPETS

The following is the actual text.

> Then the seven angels with the seven trumpets prepared to blow their mighty blasts. The first angel blew his trumpet, and hail and fire mixed with blood were thrown down on the earth. One-third of the earth was set on fire, one-third of the trees were burned, and all the green grass was burned.
>
> Then the second angel blew his trumpet, and a great mountain of fire was thrown into the sea. One-third of the water in the sea became blood, one-third of all things living in the sea died, and one-third of all the ships on the sea were destroyed.
>
> Then the third angel blew his trumpet, and a great star fell from the sky, burning like a torch. It fell on one-third of the rivers and on the springs of water. The name of the star was Bitterness. It made one-third of the water bitter, and many people died from drinking the bitter water.
>
> Then the fourth angel blew his trumpet, and one-third of the sun was struck, and one-third of the moon, and one-third of the stars, and they became dark. And one-third of the day was dark, and also one-third of the night. Then I

looked, and I heard a single eagle crying loudly as it flew through the air, "Terror, terror, terror to all who belong to this world because of what will happen when the last three angels blow their trumpets."

—Revelation 8:6–13

(The literal meaning in the Greek for the star named Bitterness is "wormwood.")

Revelation 9:
The Fifth and Sixth Trumpets

The fifth trumpet

Then the fifth angel blew his trumpet, and I saw a star that had fallen to earth from the sky, and he was given the key to the shaft of the bottomless pit. When he opened it, smoke poured out as though from a huge furnace, and the sunlight and air turned dark from the smoke. Then locusts came from the smoke and descended on the earth, and they were given power to sting like scorpions. They were told not to harm the grass or plants or trees, but only the people who did not have the seal of God on their foreheads. They were told not to kill them but to torture them for five months with pain like the pain of a scorpion sting. In those days people will seek death but will not find it. They will long to die, but death will flee from them!

The locusts looked like horses prepared for battle. They had what looked like gold crowns on their heads, and their faces looked like human faces. They had hair like women's hair and teeth like the teeth of a lion. They wore armor made of iron, and their wings roared like an army of chariots rushing into battle. They had tails that stung like scorpions, and for five months they had the power to torment people. Their king is the angel from the bottomless pit; his name in Hebrew is Abaddon, and in Greek, Apollyon—the

Destroyer. The first terror is past, but look, two more terrors are coming!

—REVELATION 9:1–12

(The bottomless pit is also known as the abyss or the underworld.)

The sixth trumpet

Then the sixth angel blew his trumpet, and I heard a voice speaking from the four horns of the gold altar that stands in the presence of God. And the voice said to the sixth angel who held the trumpet, "Release the four angels who are bound at the great Euphrates River." Then the four angels who had been prepared for this hour and day and month and year were turned loose to kill one-third of all the people on earth. I heard the size of their army, which was 200 million mounted troops.

And in my vision, I saw the horses and the riders sitting on them. The riders wore armor that was fiery red and dark blue and yellow. The horses had heads like lions, and fire and smoke and burning sulfur billowed from their mouths. One-third of all the people on earth were killed by these three plagues—by the fire and smoke and burning sulfur that came from the mouths of the horses. Their power was in their mouths and in their tails. For their tails had heads like snakes, with the power to injure people.

But the people who did not die in these plagues still refused to repent of their evil deeds and turn to God. They continued to worship demons and idols made of gold, silver, bronze, stone, and wood—idols that can neither see nor hear nor walk! And they did not repent of their murders or their witchcraft or their sexual immorality or their thefts.

—REVELATION 9:13–21

The detail in the above two passages is very descriptive but if we simplify it for the sake of clarity, it will help us to see through all the description. Let's look at the verses again.

In verses 1–2 it tells us of the star that *had* fallen. This is in the past tense so refers to a star that had fallen before the vision was given. Remember, Satan was previously an archangel known as Lucifer or a "morning star," and he was cast down to earth when he rebelled and tried to exalt himself above God. Satan took with him a multitude of angels who also rebelled against God and they were all cast down to earth (see Isaiah 14:12–15, NIV). So the star that was "given the key to the shaft of the Abyss" (Rev. 9:1, NIV) could be a fallen angel or even Satan himself. The Abyss is hell.

Verses 3–11 tell of the locusts that will come out of the Abyss to torture and torment those who are left on earth. These would be unbelievers and also complacent Christians who have not made themselves ready for Jesus' return and those who once believed but then abandoned their faith and rejected Him. The torment will go on for five months and will be so overwhelming that people will want to die but death will elude them. The description of the locusts is horrific and represents the image of everything that will be found in hell—evil, terrifying, ferocious, relentless, and merciless. The king over these demonic spirits manifesting as locusts is Satan, the destroyer, also known as Abaddon and Apollyon.

Verses 13–19 describe the release of a vast army of 200 million who will be unleashed upon the face of the earth. A third of all mankind will be killed by this army by the plagues of fire, smoke, and sulfur that come out of the mouths of the horses they are riding on. These horses will have tails like snakes that will have heads on that inflict injury. The riders will wear armor of fiery red, blue, and yellow. God's Word is very specific about this detail, and as followers of Christ we must believe Him when He says that a vast army wearing these colors will arise to destroy a third of mankind. We need to keep our eyes open and watch.

And finally, in verses 20–21 what is shocking is that the

two-thirds of mankind who are not killed by this vast army will still not repent of their evil deeds, which are listed as the works of their hands; the worship of demons; the worship of gold, silver, bronze, stone, and wood idols that cannot see, hear, or walk; murders; magic arts; sexual immorality; and thefts.

They will experience the torture and torment of the locusts for five months; survive the plagues of fire, smoke, sulfur, and injury from the two hundred million horses and their riders; and yet, despite all of this, it will not cause them to fall on their faces before God in repentance of all their sin. This could be any one of us, if we are a believer who is involved in sin that we have not confessed and repented of. Come on, church; wake up!

REVELATION 10: THE ANGEL AND THE SCROLL

Verses 1–7, summary

John sees another mighty angel descend from heaven with a scroll in his hand. When he gave a loud shout the voice of seven thunders spoke. John was about to write down what the seven thunders spoke, but a voice from heaven told him not to do this and said that what the seven thunders spoke must be sealed up. The mighty angel with the scroll lifted his right hand to heaven and declared that there would be no more delay and that when the seventh trumpet is sounded, the mysterious plan of God will be accomplished and fulfilled just as He had announced it to His servants the prophets. (See chapter 5, "What the Prophets Said.")

Verses 8–11, summary

The voice from heaven instructs John to take the scroll (which contains the sealed words of the seven thunders) out of the mighty angel's hand. He is told to eat the scroll, which will be sweet in the mouth but turn sour in the stomach. Whatever the prophetic words of the seven thunders are on the scroll, John is told to prophecy *again* about many people, nations, languages, and kings.

We can assume that this prophecy is very unpleasant in view of the effect it has on him physically.

Revelation 11: The Two Witnesses and the Seventh Trumpet

Verses 1–14, summary

For forty-two months (three and a half years) the Holy City (Jerusalem) will be trampled on by the Gentile nations. (See chapter 2 for Jesus' words in the Gospels confirming this.) At this time two end-time witnesses will appear who will prophesy for 1,260 days (i.e., forty-two months). During this time, they will have power to withhold the rain, turn water into blood, and strike the earth with every kind of plague as often as they want. If anyone tries to harm them, fire comes out of their mouths to destroy their enemies.

At the end of the 1,260 days when they finish prophesying, the beast will come out of the Abyss to kill them. Their bodies will lie in the street of the great city for three and a half days and will not be permitted burial. People from every nation, tribe, and language will come and gaze at their bodies and gloat over them and even celebrate their death by giving presents to each other, because God's two witnesses "tormented" them with their prophesying.

Suddenly, at the end of the three and a half days, God will bring them back to life and they will stand up. Terror will strike everyone who sees this. Then a loud voice from heaven will call the two witnesses up and they will ascend in a cloud while their enemies look on. At that very hour the city will be hit by a severe earthquake causing a tenth of it to collapse, and seven thousand people will die. The survivors will be terrified, but they will give glory to God.

Verses 15–19, summary

This is the seventh and final trumpet. As the angel sounds his trumpet, loud voices are heard in heaven declaring that the kingdom of the world (which became Satan's kingdom after he was cast out of heaven and down to earth because of his rebellion against God [see Isaiah 14:12–15]) has now become the kingdom of God and of Christ, who will reign forever and ever.

The twenty-four elders who are sitting on their thrones fall on their faces and worship God, proclaiming that the time has come for judging the dead; for rewarding God's servants, the prophets, the saints, and those who revere God's name; and for destroying those who cause destruction on the earth. Then John sees God's temple in heaven open and the ark of the covenant could be seen. Again there is lightning, rumbling, thunder, an earthquake and a great hailstorm.

Praise the Lord! At the blast of the seventh trumpet, the earth that is currently the dominion of Satan will be transferred in an instant from Satan's rule into the kingdom of God and of Christ, who will reign over the earth forever! Hallelujah!

REVELATION 12: THE WOMAN AND THE DRAGON

From this chapter onwards we each need to ask the Lord for even more of His wisdom in understanding the various descriptions and symbolism used throughout the text. Many believers get put off by all the symbolism and give up trying to understand it. It has taken me twenty years to get to the point of asking the Lord to help me make sense of it.

If we prayerfully seek the Lord to give us a revelation of more up-to-date words that could be used in place of the symbolic words, it will become much easier to understand. I have done this and have used the words that I feel the Lord has given me that could represent the symbolism used in the further chapters of the Book of Revelation. We must not be afraid to ask the Lord to help us to understand this vital book about the end of the world. So that readers do not get completely baffled, below is a list of the existing difficult to understand symbols and next to them I have written some up-to-date representations that could apply:

- Woman—the true Christian church

- Child—Jesus

- Offspring—followers of Christ

- Dragon—Satan

- First beast—global super state/religious system

- Second beast—the false prophet (assistant to the first beast)

- Seven heads—leaders of the global super state/religious system

- Ten horns—ten branches/kingdoms which make up the global super state

- Ten crowns—indicating that the ten horns may be ten kingdoms/nations

- Lamb—Jesus

- Saints—true believers and followers of Christ

I will insert the up-to-date words next to the existing words only once for each word, then after that I will retain the existing symbols and leave you to use the table of modern words as you read the summaries that I write.

Summary

Very briefly, it would seem that the vision John sees is a spiritual vision of the church (represented here by a woman). Her "offspring" represents all believers who follow Jesus Christ, obey the Word of God, and keep their testimony to the end.

The dragon (Satan) having not succeeded in devouring the

woman's Child (Jesus) then proceeds to go after her "offspring" (all true believers). The dragon then stands on the shore of the sea.

REVELATION 13:1-18:
THE TWO BEASTS AND THE MARK

Verses 1–15, summary

John sees a beast with seven heads, ten horns, and ten crowns on its horns rising up out of the sea. On each of the seven heads were names that blasphemed God. The dragon gives this beast his power and his throne and great authority. This beast has the power and the throne of Satan.

To me, this "beast" could represent a global superpower or super state and religious system that has immense authority over the whole world. Its "heads" (leaders) are against God (as indicated by the blasphemies). It seems to suggest an authority that has (or will have had) seven leaders up to the time to which this prophecy relates. Out of this system of heads are ten horns (or branches), each with a crown, suggesting these may be ten "kingdoms."

On the forehead of one of these seven heads (of the system) is a wound, which appears fatal but was healed. This could suggest a leader who was fatally wounded at some point but was healed. Because of this healing, the whole world marvels at it and they follow this beast. The world worships the dragon because he gave the beast his power, and they also worship the beast itself.

This beast, with authority over the world, will speak proud and blasphemous words against God, against heaven, and against those who dwell in heaven for forty-two months and will use his power and authority to wage war against God's holy people (those who have become followers of Christ during the Tribulation) and to conquer them.

This beast is so powerful that its satanic authority rules over every tribe and people and language and nation. All the people who belong to this world (those who refuse to believe in Jesus

Christ) worship the beast. Their names are not written in the Book of Life, which belongs to the Lamb that was slain (Jesus).

The saints (followers of Christ during the Tribulation) are called to patient endurance and faithfulness during this horrific time.

A second beast (the false prophet) then appears and exercises all authority on behalf of the first beast. So this may suggest that the second beast will be someone who rises to power acting on behalf of or representing the authority of the first beast. It would suggest that the first and second beast work together; but the first beast "pulls all the strings" while the second beast carries out the commands given by the first beast.

This second beast will force all the people to worship the first beast. This second beast will perform great signs and miracles on behalf of the first beast, thereby deceiving the whole world to worship and follow him. This second beast will order a statue to be made of the first beast and will give this statue life so that it can speak. This statue of the first beast then orders that anyone who does not worship it must die.

The mark of the beast

The second beast, which represents the first beast, will then force everyone—from the least to the greatest, rich and poor, slave and free—to be given a mark on their right hand or on their forehead so that no one can buy or sell anything *unless* they have this mark. This mark is the name of the beast or the number representing his name. (Receiving this mark will indicate that you belong to the beast.) Remember, Satan has given the beast his power and authority; therefore, if you receive the mark of the beast, it means you belong to Satan. Scripture exhorts us to use wisdom to solve the meaning of the number of the beast—the number of a *man* whose number is 666.

In the Greek and Roman alphabet, each letter of the alphabet has a numerical equivalent. You can use this numerical system to work out the number of your own name. You can use it to work out the number of all of Jesus' names and also the number of all of Satan's names. We must not be afraid to use technology in our search for information on this matter. It may reveal some information that will help you unravel the mysteries of all of this. Revelation 13:18 is an instruction which we need to heed and carry out, "Wisdom is needed here. Let the one with understanding *solve the meaning of the number of the beast,* for it is the number of a *man.* His number is 666" (v. 18, emphasis added). Using the Greek and Roman numerical system, our search should look for a man or the *name* of a man that represents a system of political and religious authority that embraces the whole world.

I would suggest that we do not take the subject of the mark of the beast lightly. If God should so decide that Jesus' return to rapture the true believers should occur in our lifetime, then this would mean that the Tribulation would immediately follow in our lifetime too. The scriptures show that the receiving of the mark of the beast will occur during the tribulation period. This being the case, would there be a slow, subtle, and even secretive time of preparation to produce and test various prototypes of the "mark" on the unsuspecting world that will eventually be placed on the forehead or the right hand? If so, would that not have to take place in the time period prior to the commencement of the Tribulation? I believe that these are questions we ought to ask ourselves and do some research in order to find answers.

This secret preparation could be taking place right now while we go about our daily business, unaware of how Satan is using his earthly followers to fulfill this devastating part of end-time prophecy. It has to happen at some point before the tribulation begins, so it could easily be happening now. But it would appear that many prefer to remain in ignorance of these things, perhaps because they may seem too far-fetched like something out of a sci-fi movie; and so they close their eyes and minds to its possibility. We need to overcome our narrow-minded mindset on this issue, and bravely go on the search to solve the meaning of the number of the beast and research the possibility of versions of the mark already being produced and even tested out on unsuspecting individuals. We have the technology to find answers.

Revelation 14: The Lamb and the 144,000, the Three Angels, and the Harvests

Verses 1–5, summary

This refers to the 144,000, which I mentioned earlier in Revelation chapter 7. These are the ones who have kept themselves as pure as virgins, have never lied, and are blameless. They have the name of God, the name of the Lamb, and the seal of God on their foreheads, and they will stand with the Lamb on Mount Zion. A great choir of angels sings a wonderful new song in front of God's throne and only these 144,000 are able to learn it. They follow the Lamb wherever He goes. They have been redeemed from the earth as a special offering to God and to the Lamb.

Verses 6–13, summary

John sees three angels making proclamations. The first angel proclaims the eternal gospel to all the peoples of every nation, tribe, and language, telling them to fear God and give Him glory because the hour of God's judgment has come.

Remember Jesus' words in the Gospels saying that the gospel must be preached in every nation and then the end will come (Matt. 24:14)? At this critical point, even one of God's holy angels is proclaiming the gospel of salvation to the whole world. The Lord, in His great mercy, does not want anyone to perish (2 Pet. 3:9) and is giving the whole of mankind one last opportunity to repent of their sins and put their faith in Jesus Christ to be saved.

The second angel declares that Babylon has fallen, the great city that made all the nations drink the wine of her adulteries. (See the description of Babylon in Revelation 17.)

The third angel declares that if anyone worships the beast and the statue of the beast and receives the mark of the beast on their hand or forehead, they will also receive the wrath of God which has been poured out full strength into His cup of wrath and they will be tormented with burning sulfur in the presence of the holy angels and the Lamb, and the smoke of their torment will rise forever and ever. There is no rest day or night for those who worship the beast and his statue, or for anyone who receives the mark of his name.

Those who are God's children, who obey God's commandments and remain faithful to Jesus, must patiently endure this horrific time. I believe these children of God are the ones who become followers of Christ during the Tribulation, and also those who were *not* ready when Jesus returned to rapture the true believers. These children of God are the ones who are left behind to endure the horrors of the Tribulation because of their failure to obey Jesus' word to keep watch for His return and to be ready at His appearing. Having been left behind, they have come to their senses and have repented and turned back to believing and following Jesus prior to the end of the world.

John then hears a voice from heaven that tells him to write these words, "Blessed are those who die in the Lord from now on. Yes, says the Spirit, they are blessed indeed, for they will rest from their hard work; for their good deeds will follow them!" (v. 13). This could indicate that from that point on, anyone who is a believer or becomes a believer during the Tribulation may be put to death as a result of having faith in the Lord.

Verses 14–20, summary

It seems that two harvests then take place. The first harvest is by a person on a white cloud who appears like the Son of Man with a gold crown on His head. An angel from the temple of God calls to Him loudly to swing the sharp sickle in His hand and reap the harvest of the earth because the time has come. This seems to be the final gathering up of all the previously lukewarm, complacent believers who had been left behind on earth at the Rapture and have now repented, and also any unbelievers who have turned to Christ during the Tribulation. At this point all true believers are now safely with the Lord.

The second harvest is carried out by an angel who comes out of the temple, also holding a sharp sickle in his hand. Another angel calls loudly to this angel to take his sickle and gather the clusters of grapes from the earth's vine; he does this and throws its grapes into the winepress of God's wrath where they will be trampled in the winepress outside the city. Their blood will flow out of the press rising up to the height of a horse's bridle for a distance of 180 miles. This is not some fantasy horror story. It is a *real* horror story that is *really* going to happen. This angel would seem to be the "grim reaper" that comes to destroy all those who have not believed in God or His Son, Jesus Christ, as we will see in the following passages.

REVELATION 15: THE SEVEN ANGELS WITH SEVEN PLAGUES

Summary

After all of what we have just read so far, things intensify even more on the earth, which now has only unbelievers and also *unrepentant* believers left on it (after the final gathering up of the remaining repentant believers in Revelation 14). The following things will be happening on the earth right up to the final end of the world.

John sees seven angels with the last seven plagues. They are the last ones because they complete God's wrath upon all those who refuse to believe in His Son, Jesus Christ, as we shall see in Revelation 16. But before the angels pour out these plagues, John sees all those who have been victorious over the beast and his statue and over the number representing his name. They are standing beside a sea that looks like glass mixed with fire. They hold harps that God has given them, and they sing the song of Moses and the song of the Lamb.

After this John sees the temple of God opened, and out of the temple come the seven angels dressed in clean, shining linen with golden sashes around their chests. One of the four living creatures gives the seven angels the seven bowls filled with the wrath of God (the last seven plagues). The temple is filled with smoke from the glory of God and from His power. No one could enter the temple until the seven plagues were completed.

Revelation 16: The Last Seven Plagues

Summary

John hears a loud voice from the temple telling the seven angels to pour out the seven bowls of God's wrath onto the earth. The first angel pours out his bowl onto the earth and painful, ugly sores break out on everyone who has the mark of the beast and who worship his image. The second angel pours out his bowl onto the sea and it turns into blood, and every living thing in the sea dies. The third angel pours out his bowl on the rivers and springs of water and they turn to blood too.

John then hears the angel, who is in charge of the waters, say,

> "You are just, O Holy One, who is and who always was, because you have sent these judgments. Since they shed the blood of your holy people and your prophets, you have given them blood to drink. It is their just reward." And I heard a voice from the altar, saying, "Yes, O Lord God, the Almighty, your judgments are true and just."
>
> —Revelation 16:5–7

The fourth angel pours out his bowl on the sun, and it was given power to scorch people with fire. They curse the name of God who has control over these plagues, *but they refuse to repent of their sins and give glory to God.* The fifth angel pours out his bowl on the throne of the beast, and the beast's kingdom was plunged into darkness. The people gnaw their tongues in agony because of their pains and their sores, *but still they refuse to repent of what they have done.* The sixth angel pours out his bowl on the great river Euphrates and its waters dry up to prepare the way for the kings of the east to come for the final battle at the place called Armageddon. Three evil spirits that look like frogs come out of the mouth of the dragon and out of the mouth of the beast and out of the mouth of the false prophet. These evil froglike spirits are demons that perform miraculous signs, and they go out to the kings of the whole world to gather them for the battle on the great day of God Almighty.

The Lamb speaks and says, "Look, I will come as unexpectedly as a thief! Blessed are all who are watching for me, who keep their clothing ready so they will not have to walk around naked and ashamed" (v. 15).

The three evil spirits gather the kings together at the place called Armageddon.

The seventh angel pours out his bowl into the air and a loud voice comes out of the temple from the throne saying, "It is finished!" Then there is lightning and rumbling, the like of which has never occurred since man has been on the earth. The great city splits into three sections and the cities of the nations collapse into heaps of rubble. God remembers Babylon's sins and makes her drink the cup of the wine of His fierce wrath. All the islands disappear and the mountains are leveled. Huge hailstones, each weighing about a hundred pounds, fall from the sky upon the people and they curse God because this plague is so terrible.

God's Word has said all these things *will* happen, so therefore we need to accept it and believe it and not deceive ourselves or other believers that this is all just a fanciful, symbolic story which won't *really* happen like this. God has said in His Word, "This is my dearly beloved Son, who brings me great joy. *Listen to Him*" (Matt. 17:5, emphasis added).

REVELATION 17: THE GREAT PROSTITUTE

Summary

One of the seven angels shows John the judgment that is going to come upon the great "prostitute" who rules over many waters. The kings of the earth have committed adultery with this great prostitute and the people of the earth are intoxicated with the wine of her adulteries.

The angel shows John a woman (who is the great prostitute) sitting on a scarlet beast that has seven heads and ten horns and it has blasphemies against God all over it (the same beast and the same horns mentioned in Revelation chapter 13). This woman is dressed in purple and scarlet and has jewelry of gold and precious gems and pearls (again mentioned in Revelation 13). In her hand is a golden cup filled with abominable things and the filth of her adulteries. On this woman's forehead is written a name that is a mystery, "Babylon the Great, the Mother of Prostitutes and of the Abominations of the Earth" (v. 5, NIV). (Note: This 'woman' is *not* the same 'woman' mentioned in Revelation chapter 12.)

The woman is drunk with the blood of the saints, those who bear testimony of Jesus. (The beast that the woman sits upon murders and has murdered true believers, probably many millions throughout the centuries. I would encourage all readers to do some thorough research as to what system, in the present time we live in would fit all the descriptions contained in this chapter.) John is astonished at what he is seeing, and so the angel explains to him the mystery of the woman and the beast she is sitting on.

I will start with the woman in verse 18. The woman is the great city that rules over the kings of the earth. The word *woman* is often used to refer to the church or a religious system. The true church of believers is known as the bride of Christ. But this woman, known as the great prostitute, could suggest a religious system that appears to be in the form of a church that outwardly looks godly and appears to be following Christ, thereby attracting and deceiving many people from all nations, tribes, and languages. But inwardly its root is not in Christ at all but belongs to the beast (Satan). This religious system may use the words *God, Christ,* and *Jesus* and may outwardly go through the religious motions and rituals to display a form of holiness, but nonetheless it is a deception.

Remember, Satan's purpose is to deceive the whole world into following him, and what better way to do it than through something that looks like a church and displays a form of holiness and godliness. Satan is not going to make it obvious to the world that it is him who is deceiving them. A deception is something that looks like the real thing but in fact is a lie. It is a counterfeit. Think of counterfeit money; sometimes the fake money is so well produced that even the experts are fooled into believing it is the real thing. This is what Satan is doing by creating a global religious system that looks like the real thing but is in fact a counterfeit.

So this woman on the beast appears to be some sort of organization that seems religious on the outside, and it rules over the kings of the earth. This woman wears purple and scarlet clothing and is decked with gold, silver, precious stones, and pearls and holds a gold goblet in her hand. As believers we need to do research to see if there is a religious system in our present time that fits this description.

The waters where this woman sits or rules (referred to in verse 15 and also verse 1) represent masses of peoples of every nation and language. This woman sits on or rules over a vast majority of peoples from all nations of the world. We need to remember that this is a prophecy concerning the end-time period that was being shown to the apostle John in a vision—a vision that would be fulfilled at an appointed time long after John's death and would refer to people and situations that had not yet occurred at the time the vision was given to him.

The angel describes the beast as someone who was once alive but died, yet he will soon come alive again. The people of the world, whose names are not written in the Book of Life, will be amazed at the reappearance of this beast that had died. The seven heads of the beast represent the seven hills where the woman (religious system) rules. This beast rules from its "headquarters" among seven hills. These seven heads also represent kings. Five had already been and gone, the sixth was reigning, and the seventh was yet to come and would reign for only a brief period. After the seventh king has had his brief reign, the scarlet beast that was once alive but had died will reappear and become the eighth (and final) king. The angel says that he is like the other seven heads. So to me this indicates someone who takes over from the previous heads. Each of these heads, in succession, fulfils a role on the earth with great power and authority over multitudes of peoples from all the nations of the earth. The angel says that the beast "is headed for destruction" (v. 11).

The angel says, "This calls for a mind with understanding" (v. 9), so we must pray to the Lord and ask Him to give us wisdom and knowledge concerning these very specific things. We must not be afraid to search for answers. God will lead us to what He wants us to discover that fits the descriptions revealed in the vision given to the apostle John.

In verse 3 the angel says that this woman *is sitting on* the beast with the ten horns. Again, we could interpret the phrase "sitting on" to mean "ruling over." This beast rules over the ten horns. If we refer back to my summary of Revelation chapter 13, you will see that the ten horns could refer to ten kingdoms with ten kings represented by the ten crowns mentioned in Revelation 13:1. Indeed, in Revelation 17:12, God's Word confirms that the ten horns of the beast are ten kings who had not yet risen to power at the time that John was given this vision. The ten kings will rise to power and be appointed to their kingdoms for one brief moment to reign with the beast. *All these ten kings will agree to give the beast their power and their authority.*

Have we grasped this? Ten kingdoms will suddenly rise for a

brief time, giving all their power and authority to the beast that is their "head" and rules over them. Whatever power and authority they have as kingdoms, they will just agree to give over to the beast. The purpose of this is so that the beast will use his great authority over the nations and, together with the ten horns, will go to war against the Lamb. But the Lamb will defeat them because He is the Lord of all lords and the King of all kings, and His chosen and faithful ones will be with Him. We will see this battle take place at Armageddon, as described further ahead in Revelation 19.

In Revelation 17:7 it says that the woman who wears the purple and scarlet clothing *sits* on the beast, so again we could interpret this to mean that this woman actually rules over the beast, even though the beast has been given Satan's power and authority (see Revelation 13:2). So it would seem that this woman is actually pulling the strings of the beast, getting it to do what *she* wants.

In verse 16, it says that the beast and his ten horns actually all hate the woman that sits on them and so they will strip her naked, eat her flesh, and burn her remains with fire. Verse 17 says that God has actually put this plan into their minds to carry out the fulfillment of His purposes. We will see the eventual destruction of this mysterious woman, Babylon the Great, in the chapter below.

REVELATION 18:
THE FALL OF BABYLON

Summary

This is a graphic description of the fall and destruction of the "great city" Babylon at the hand of God's wrath. It becomes a home for demons and every foul spirit and every foul and dreadful animal. This city exalted itself on its throne and all the nations fell because they grew rich due to this city's extravagant luxury. The nations of the world supplied everything that this city needed, and now it is brought to ruin and all the nations mourn at its sudden destruction. As they see the smoke rise, they are terrified.

The nations of the world supplied this city with great quantities of gold, silver, jewels, pearls, purple and scarlet cloth, silk, ivory goods, objects made from expensive wood, marble, bronze, iron, and many other things, including human slaves. This deceiving city deals in human trafficking. Again, research is needed. The city that is involved in human trafficking is the "woman" mentioned in Revelation 17, who is clothed in the finest purple and scarlet linen and decked with gold, silver, precious stones, and pearls.

But the city's destruction has come. In a single moment it is all gone, and the world looks on in astonishment. This city deceived the nations with its sorceries or trickeries. This city's streets flow with the blood of the prophets of God and of God's holy people and the blood of people slaughtered all over the world. This could suggest that this city is responsible for mass murder of God's prophets and followers throughout history, including the slaughter of other people all over the world. (Perhaps genocide or ethnic cleansing?) God's Word indicates that this city is responsible for a massacre of global proportions. Again, research is called for.

In verse 20 the people of God, the apostles, and the whole of heaven are told to rejoice over the destruction of this city, for at last God has judged it for their sakes. This city will never be found again. Nothing will ever be heard in it ever again. It will cease to exist.

REVELATION 19: SHOUTING IN HEAVEN AND THE WHITE HORSE RIDER

Verses 1–10, summary

John then hears what sounds like a vast crowd in heaven shouting praises to the Lord for the destruction of this great city that corrupted the whole world with its immorality. The twenty-four elders and the four living creatures fall down and worship God.

Then John hears more shouting in heaven, praising the Lord

who reigns and exhorting us to "'be glad and rejoice for the time has come for the wedding feast of the Lamb, *and his bride has prepared herself.* She has been given the finest of pure white linen to wear.' For the fine linen represents the good deeds of God's holy people" (vv. 7–8, emphasis added). These good deeds are not only the good things we do, such as helping others. They are also the good deeds of the way we live our life in Christ right up to the moment we physically die or when He returns (whichever comes first). The state of our heart, the thoughts of our mind, and our attitudes and motives—these all represent our deeds. If we examine our deeds, will we find them to be good or bad?

In verse 9 the angel of the Lord says, "Blessed are those who are *invited* to the wedding feast of the Lamb" (emphasis added). This word *invited* is very important and has been greatly overlooked in today's church. God's Word tells us that *everyone will not* end up in heaven when they die. Those who will make it into heaven are *invited.* That invitation from God is the gospel message of salvation through faith in His Son, Jesus Christ, the Bridegroom to whom the invitation relates. God freely distributes this wedding invitation of salvation through faith in Jesus Christ to the whole of mankind from every nation, tribe, and language through the witness of the true followers of Jesus Christ.

The invitation is given; *but* just because you have received an invitation does not automatically give you the right to expect entry to the wedding. You have to *respond* to the invitation. You have to let the One who sent you the invitation know that you wish to come *and that you will be ready* when the day of the wedding arrives. Only then will a place be set for you at the table. If you do not respond to the invitation or you respond by actually declining the invitation, a place will not be set for you at the table of the wedding feast.

Stephanie Cottam puts this very strongly, and rightly so, because it is a very serious matter to not respond to the invitation or to decline it altogether. She writes,

If you are going to decline the ultimate invitation to the greatest wedding you could ever have the pleasure of attending, you need to make sure you know exactly what you are saying...Be sure you know what it is you are rejecting. Understand who it is you will need to give your RSVP back to, and how you will face Him when you see Him after you have given your rejection.

I can assure you of this one truth. Nothing you think you can offer as a good enough reason for saying "No, thank you" will actually stand up before God. You haven't only rejected His invitation to attend the wedding of His Son Jesus Christ, you have rejected His invitation as the Bride of Christ. You have rejected His offer of love, forgiveness, the removal of your sins, but more importantly, you are rejecting His offer to spend eternity with Him.[2]

In verse 10, John falls at the feet of the angel to worship him, but the angel rebukes him and tells John not to do this as the angel is a servant of God just like John and his brothers and sisters who testify about their faith in Jesus (i.e., all true believers). The angel tells John to worship only God and that the essence of prophecy is to give a clear witness for Jesus.

The rider on the white horse

Then I saw heaven opened, and a white horse was standing there. Its rider was named Faithful and True, for he judges fairly and wages a righteous war. His eyes were like flames of fire, and on his head were many crowns. A name was written on him that no one understood except himself. He wore a robe dipped in blood, and his title was the Word of God. The armies of heaven, dressed in the finest of pure white linen, followed him on white horses. From his mouth came a sharp sword to strike down the nations. He will rule them with an iron rod. He will release the fierce wrath of God, the Almighty, like juice flowing from a winepress. On his robe at his thigh was written this title: King of all kings and Lord of all lords.

Then I saw an angel standing in the sun, shouting to the vultures flying high in the sky: "Come! Gather together for the great banquet God has prepared. Come and eat the flesh of kings, generals, and strong warriors; of horses and their riders; and of all humanity, both free and slave, small and great."

Then I saw the beast and the kings of the world and their armies gathered together to fight against the one sitting on the horse and his army. And the beast was captured, and with him the false prophet who did mighty miracles on behalf of the beast—miracles that deceived all who had accepted the mark of the beast and who worshiped his statue. Both the beast and his false prophet were thrown alive into the fiery lake of burning sulfur. Their entire army was killed by the sharp sword that came from the mouth of the one riding the white horse. And the vultures all gorged themselves on the dead bodies.

—REVELATION 19:11–21

We know without a doubt that this rider on the white horse is Jesus, as He is Faithful and True. He is the Word of God and the Word made flesh (see John 1:1, 14). He is the King of all kings and the Lord of all lords.

This is the great battle of the beast, the false prophet, and the kings and generals and strong warriors of the world against the Son of God and the armies of heaven at the place called Armageddon, previously referred to in Revelation 16:16. The beast and his false prophet are thrown alive into the lake of burning sulfur.

Their whole army is killed by the sword that comes out of the mouth of the One riding on the white horse. If we remember, Jesus is the Word of God and the Sword of the Spirit is the Word of God. Therefore, the sword that comes out of Jesus' mouth is the

Word of God, and it is this Word that destroys the beast's and the false prophet's entire army.

REVELATION 20: THE THOUSAND YEARS, SATAN'S DEFEAT, AND THE FINAL JUDGMENT

Verses 1–6, summary

After the Word of God that comes out of the mouth of Jesus has destroyed the army of the beast and the false prophet, an angel binds Satan in chains for a thousand years and throws him into the bottomless pit (Abyss), locking it so that he can no longer deceive the nations. After the thousand years are finished, Satan will be released for a short time.

John then sees people sitting on thrones who are given authority to judge. He sees the souls of all who have been beheaded for their faith, their testimony about Jesus, and proclaiming the Word of God. These are the ones who have not worshiped the beast or his statue and who have not accepted his mark on their right hand or their forehead. All these souls (which had been beheaded for their faith in Jesus Christ) come back to life again and reign with Jesus for the thousand years.

This is known as the first resurrection. Those who share in the first resurrection are blessed and holy because the second death holds no power over them. (The second death is the lake of fire, which will be mentioned in Revelation 20:11–15.)

God's Word says that the rest of the dead (i.e., those who have *not* been beheaded for their faith and testimony of Jesus, but have died a natural death) will not come back to life until *after* the thousand years of Jesus' reign is ended (v. 5).

Verses 7–10, summary

As we have seen in Revelation 19:19–21, the beast and his false prophet were thrown alive into the lake of fire following the destruction of their entire army; but now Satan is about to receive his eternal punishment. However, just prior to this at the end of the thousand years, Satan is let out of the bottomless pit to deceive everyone from the nations called Gog and Magog and will gather them together from wherever they are around the world for the final battle against the Lord's people and His beloved city Jerusalem.

If we look at Ezekiel 38, we will see in verses 1–2 That Gog is a person of the land of Magog and is a prince who rules over the nations of Meshech and Tubal. In Genesis 10:2 we find that Magog, Meshech, and Tubal are sons of Japheth (one of Noah's sons), so these names really relate to the descendants of Magog, Meshech, and Tubal rather than the names of nations.

We would need to do a thorough research to establish the modern names of the nations that are the lands occupied by the descendants of Magog, Meshech, and Tubal. I have attempted to do this for my own understanding, and I found some evidence as to who these modern day nations may be. There are nations in existence which would seem to fit the descriptions of these end-time nations who will come against God's beloved city Jerusalem.

But we need to remember that while this battle appears to be waged against God's people, this battle is actually that of the anti-christ (Satan) against Jesus Christ, the Son of God, the Messiah. Satan already knows that he will meet his final defeat in this battle against the Lord Jesus Christ and that his ultimate end will be in the lake of burning sulfur (Rev. 20:10). But Satan still wants to deceive the whole world into thinking that he, along with his army of earthly followers, can defeat the Messiah in this final battle of all battles.

The army mentioned in verses 7–10 will be as many as the grains of sand on the seashore. They will march across the earth and surround God's people and the beloved city. But fire will come down from heaven and consume them. Satan will finally be thrown into the lake of fire, joining the beast and his false prophet, where they will be tormented day and night forever and ever.

As believers we need to wake up out of our complacent slumber where end-time events are concerned. Time could be short. Jesus is coming back, and we do not want to be found half asleep, caught unawares because we were too lazy to make the effort to remain alert and watchful for the signs on the earth of His approaching return and the events which will lead up to this final battle of the end of the world. We must not allow confusion and our own lack of understanding to put us off from finding out where we are at in relation to the end times that Jesus has warned us will come upon the whole world.

Verses 11–15, summary

With the thousand years now passed and all the dead now raised (see Revelation 20:5), John now sees a great white throne and the One who sits on it. All the dead, both great and small, are standing before God's throne and books are opened, including the Book of Life. "All the dead were judged according to what they had done, as recorded in the books.... All are judged according to their deeds" (v. 12–13).

Death and the grave are thrown into the lake of fire. There is no longer any need for either of them because the souls of all mankind will now live forever—either in the kingdom of heaven for true believers or for eternity in hell for unbelievers and backslidden, unrepentant believers who refuse to forsake the sins they are allowing to remain in their lives. There will be no more death and so there will be no need for graves; hence, both death and the grave are thrown into the lake of fire.

The lake of fire is the second death, and anyone whose name is not recorded in the Book of Life will be thrown into the lake of fire.

Revelation 21: A New Heaven, New Earth, and New Jerusalem

Summary

Now that every form of evil has been thrown into the lake of fire, John is then shown the glory and beauty of the new heaven and the new earth. It is full of the light of God and the Lamb. The gates are never shut but nothing evil will be allowed to enter it. Only those whose names are written in the Lamb's Book of Life will be permitted entry.

The New Jerusalem is colossal in its size. Its walls are two hundred sixteen feet thick and the whole city is a square that is fourteen hundred miles in width, in length, and in height. That is a massive city! The walls are made of jasper and the city is pure gold, which is like glass in its appearance. The twelve foundation stones are laid with all sorts of precious stones, and the names of the twelve apostles are written on the foundation stones. The twelve gates are made from pearl and the street is made of pure gold like glass. Twelve angels guard the gates, and the names of the twelve tribes of Israel are written on the gates.

This beautiful place is the inheritance of God's true believers, where they will live for eternity. God will wipe away every tear from their eyes and there will be no more death or sorrow or crying or pain for all those who will live there; the ones whose names are written in the Lamb's Book of Life.

Revelation 22: Trustworthy and True, Jesus Is Coming Soon

Summary

The river of life flows from the throne of God and the Lamb, down the center of the main street. On each side of the river grows the tree of life, which bears a new crop of fruit each month.

The leaves of these trees are used for healing the nations (v. 2). I would point out that I do not profess to know what the Lord means in this verse, but the Lord has stated it, so that is all that matters to me.

The angel tells John that all the things he has seen are trustworthy and true. The angel finishes by telling John that the *Lord God*, who inspires His prophets, *has sent His angel to tell His servants* (that is every Christian) *what will happen soon.*

So this incredible vision, recorded from the beginning of Revelation chapter 4 to the end of Revelation chapter 21, is the angel of God showing *us* through the apostle John's faithful account what will happen soon. The angel of God is saying that this prophetic vision of the end of the world *is* trustworthy and true.

We need to believe it, every single bit of it, including what may happen to believers who have backslidden and turned away from obedience to the Lord and returned to their previous sinful lifestyles. In some cases, what they turn back to is even worse than what they did before.

God's Word is the truth, the whole truth and nothing but the truth, so help us God. Jesus speaks, saying, "Look, I am coming soon! Blessed are those who obey the words of prophecy written in this book" (v. 7).

John again falls down at the feet of an angel to worship him, and again the angel rebukes him and tells him to worship only God. *The angel then instructs John not to seal up the prophetic words in this book, for the time of their fulfillment is near.*

According to the angel's instruction to the apostle John, the whole of the prophetic words of the Book of Revelation are now open, ready to be fulfilled. They have been open and ready to be fulfilled since the time that the vision was given to the apostle John. These end-time visions given to John have not been sealed up for a future appointed time. It would seem that the sealed end-time prophecies given in the Old Testament to the prophet Daniel were again revealed to the apostle John, and this final angel instructs John *not* to seal them up again. That would mean the end-time prophecies in the Book of Revelation are at this moment unsealed; they are open and ready to be fulfilled the moment God commands it.

Jesus speaks again,

> "Look, I am coming soon, bringing my reward with me to repay all people according to their deeds. I am the Alpha and the Omega, the First and the Last, the Beginning and the End." Blessed are those who wash their robes. They will be permitted to enter through the gates of the city and eat the fruit from the tree of life. Outside the city are the dogs—the sorcerers, the sexually immoral, the murderers, the idol worshipers, and all who love to live a lie.
>
> *"I, Jesus, have sent my angel to give you this message for the churches.* I am both the source of David and the heir to his throne. I am the bright morning star."
>
> The Spirit and the bride say, "Come." Let anyone who hears this say, "Come." Let anyone who is thirsty come. Let anyone who desires drink freely from the water of life. And I solemnly declare to everyone who hears the words of prophecy written in this book: If anyone adds anything to what is written here, God will add to that person the plagues described in this book. And if anyone removes any of the words from this book of prophecy, God will remove that person's share in the tree of life and in the holy city that are described in this book. He who is the faithful witness to all these things says, "Yes, I am coming soon!" Amen! Come, Lord Jesus!
>
> —REVELATION 22:12–20, EMPHASIS ADDED

I have emphasized some of Jesus' words in the above passage because He says that He has sent His angel to give His message to the churches. That must therefore include the church today. So why is the church now ignoring His message concerning the end of the world and His warning of eternity in hell, which many will find themselves in? The church needs to repent and wake up before it is too late.

As I have said previously, I have written this chapter of the book mainly in summaries of each chapter of the Book of Revelation, not with any intention of removing anything from it. I strongly urge you to read the full Bible text of each chapter in your own Bible. The descriptions I have written are my own understanding of things after prayer for wisdom, and further research on the issues. My personal descriptions are in no way intended to add anything to the Book of Revelation.

However, I feel that each one of us needs to seek the Lord for wisdom on the meanings and events of the Book of Revelation. But I am certain that many believers are too afraid to do any research about it in case they put themselves at risk of adding plagues to their life (see v. 18) or having God remove their share in the tree of life and in the Holy City (see v. 19).

I don't think the Lord wants us be afraid to study the subject of end-time prophecy and to close our minds to all that is contained in the amazing Book of Revelation. He has said that we are to use wisdom to understand things. Remaining with blinders on out of fear and ignorance is not what the Lord wants us to do. We need to study and find things out, but then we can present our findings to the Lord for further wisdom and understanding. Let us not be afraid to seek the Lord for His guidance regarding this vitally important book about the end of the world. What we should not do is ignore the reality and the truth of the end of the world and just idly carry on with our life on earth as though the issue of the end of the world is irrelevant to us. This is foolish and could result in catastrophic eternal consequences for us.

In His own words, Jesus says, "I am coming soon!" (v. 20). How soon? Only the Lord God knows. The angels don't know; not even Jesus knows (Matt. 24:36). But nevertheless, Jesus is saying that He is coming soon. "Soon" could be today, tomorrow, next week, next month, next year, or even many years ahead. No one knows; only the Father.

Let us honor our heavenly Father in reverential fear of His justice and His holiness and worship Him by keeping watch for the return of our Bridegroom, His beloved Son, Jesus Christ, our Lord and Savior.

Chapter 4
WHAT THE APOSTLES SAID

HAVING HEARD WHAT Jesus has to say about the end of the world, let us now look at what some of the apostles wrote on this subject. As we will see, the things that Jesus has said in the Gospels and the Book of Revelation are confirmed by the apostles and taught to the believers.

They, too, exhort the believers to live their Christian lives in keeping with God's Word, to ensure that they are watching and waiting for Jesus' return and are doing all that is necessary to be ready at His appearing.

And now, dear brothers and sisters, we want you to know what will happen to the believers who have died so you will not grieve like people who have no hope. For since we believe that Jesus died and was raised to life again, we also believe that when Jesus returns, God will bring back with him the believers who have died.

We tell you this directly from the Lord: We who are still living when the Lord returns will not meet him ahead of those who have died. For the Lord himself will come down from heaven with a commanding shout, with the voice of the archangel, and with the trumpet call of God. First, the Christians who have died will rise from their graves. Then, together with them, we who are still alive and remain on the earth will be caught up in the clouds to meet the Lord in the air. Then we will be with the Lord forever. So encourage each other with these words. Now concerning how and when all this will happen, dear brothers and sisters, we don't really need to write you. For you know quite well that the day of the Lord's return will come unexpectedly, like a thief in the night. When people are saying, "Everything is peaceful and secure," then disaster will fall on them as suddenly as a pregnant woman's labor pains begin. And there will be no escape.

But you aren't in the dark about these things, dear brothers and sisters, and you won't be surprised when the day of the Lord comes like a thief. For you are all children of the light and of the day; we don't belong to darkness and night. So be on your guard, not asleep like the others. Stay alert and be clearheaded. Night is the time when people sleep and drinkers get drunk. But let us who live in the light be clearheaded, protected by the armor of faith and love, and wearing as our helmet the confidence of our salvation. For God chose to save us through our Lord Jesus Christ, not to pour out his anger on us. Christ died for us so that, whether we are dead or alive when he returns, we can live with him forever. So encourage each other and build each other up, just as you are already doing.

—1 THESSALONIANS 4:13–5:11

We proudly tell God's other churches about your endurance and faithfulness in all the persecutions and hardships you are suffering. And God will use this persecution to show his justice and to make you worthy of his Kingdom, for which you are suffering. In his justice he will pay back those who persecute you. And God will provide rest for you who are being persecuted and also for us when the Lord Jesus appears from heaven. He will come with his mighty angels, in flaming fire, bringing judgment on those who don't know God and on those who refuse to obey the Good News of our Lord Jesus. They will be punished with eternal destruction, forever separated from the Lord and from his glorious power. When he comes on that day, he will receive glory from his holy people—praise from all who believe. And this includes you, for you believed what we told you about him. So we keep on praying for you, asking our God to enable you to live a life worthy of his call.

—2 Thessalonians 1:4–11a

Now, dear brothers and sisters, let us clarify some things about the coming of our Lord Jesus Christ and how we will be gathered to meet him. Don't be so easily shaken or alarmed by those who say that the day of the Lord has already begun. Don't believe them, even if they claim to have had a spiritual vision, a revelation, or a letter supposedly from us. Don't be fooled by what they say. For that day will not come until there is a great rebellion against God and the man of lawlessness is revealed—the one who brings destruction. He will exalt himself and defy everything that people call god and every object of worship. He will even sit in the temple of God, claiming that he himself is God.

Don't you remember that I told you about all this when I was with you? And you know what is holding him back, for he can be revealed only when his time comes. For this lawlessness is already at work secretly, and it will remain secret until the one who is holding it back steps out of the way. Then the man of lawlessness will be revealed, but the Lord Jesus will kill him with the breath of his mouth and destroy him by the splendor of his coming. This man will come to do the work of Satan with counterfeit power and signs and miracles. He will use every kind of evil deception to fool those on their way to destruction, because they refuse to love and accept the truth that would save them. So God will cause them to be greatly deceived, and they will believe these lies. Then they will be condemned for enjoying evil rather than believing the truth.

—2 Thessalonians 2:1–12

Praise be to the God and Father of our Lord Jesus Christ! In his great mercy he has given us new birth into a living hope through the resurrection of Jesus Christ from the dead, and into an inheritance that can never perish, spoil or fade. This inheritance is kept in heaven for you, who through faith are shielded by God's power until the coming of the salvation that is ready to be revealed in the last time. In all this you greatly rejoice, though now for a little while you may have had to suffer grief in all kinds of trials. These have come so that the proven genuineness of your faith—of greater worth than gold, which perishes even though refined by fire— may result in praise, glory and honor when Jesus Christ is revealed. Though you have not seen him, you love him; and even though you do not see him now, you believe in him and are filled with an inexpressible and glorious joy, for you are receiving the end result of your faith, the salvation of your souls.

Concerning this salvation, the prophets, who spoke of the grace that was to come to you, searched intently and with the greatest care, trying to find out the time and circumstances to which the Spirit of Christ in them was pointing when he predicted the sufferings of the Messiah and the glories that would follow. It was revealed to them that they were not serving themselves but you, when they spoke of the things that have now been told you by those who have preached the gospel to you by the Holy Spirit sent from heaven. Even angels long to look into these things.

Therefore, with minds that are alert and fully sober, set your hope on the grace to be brought to you when Jesus Christ is revealed at his coming. As obedient children, do not conform to the evil desires you had when you lived in ignorance. But just as he who called you is holy, so be holy in all you do; for it is written: "Be holy, because I am holy." Since you call on a Father who judges each person's work impartially, live out your time as foreigners here in reverent fear. For you know that it was not with perishable things such as silver or gold that you were redeemed from the empty way of life handed down to you from your ancestors, but with the precious blood of Christ, a lamb without blemish or defect. He was chosen before the creation of the world, but was revealed in these last times for your sake. Through him you believe in God, who raised him from the dead and glorified him, and so your faith and hope are in God. Now that you have purified yourselves by obeying the truth so that you have sincere love for each other, love one another deeply, from the heart.

For you have been born again, not of perishable seed, but of imperishable, through the living and enduring word of God. For, "All people are like grass, and all their glory is like the flowers of the field; the grass withers and the flowers fall, but the word of the Lord endures forever." And this is the word that was preached to you. Therefore, rid yourselves of all malice and all deceit, hypocrisy, envy, and slander of every kind.

—1 Peter 1:3–2:1, niv

But there were also false prophets in Israel, just as there will be false teachers among you. They will cleverly teach destructive heresies and even deny the Master who bought them. In this way, they will bring sudden destruction on themselves. Many will follow their evil teaching and shameful immorality. And because of these teachers, the way of truth will be slandered.

—2 Peter 2:1–2

Most importantly, I want to remind you that in the last days scoffers will come, mocking the truth and following their own desires. They will say, "What happened to the promise that Jesus is coming again? From before the times of our ancestors, everything has remained the same since the world was first created." They deliberately forget that God made the heavens by the word of his command, and he brought the earth out from the water and surrounded it with water. Then he used the water to destroy the ancient world with a mighty flood. And by the same word, the present heavens and earth have been stored up for fire. They are being kept for the day of judgment, when ungodly people will be destroyed.

But you must not forget this one thing, dear friends: A day is like a thousand years to the Lord, and a thousand years is like a day. The Lord isn't really being slow about his promise, as some people think. No, he is being patient for your sake. He does not want anyone to be destroyed, but wants everyone to repent. But the day of the Lord will come as unexpectedly as a thief. Then the heavens will pass away with a terrible noise, and the very elements themselves will disappear in fire, and the earth and everything on it will be found to deserve judgment. Since everything around us is going to be destroyed like this, what holy and godly lives you should live looking forward to the day of God and hurrying it along. On that day, he will set the heavens on fire, and the elements will melt away in the flames. But we are looking forward to the new heavens and new earth he has promised, a world filled with God's righteousness.

And so, dear friends, while you are waiting for these things to happen, make every effort to be found living peaceful lives that are pure and blameless in his sight. And remember, our Lord's patience gives people time to be saved. This is what our beloved brother Paul also wrote to you with the wisdom God gave him—speaking of these things in all of his letters. Some of his comments are hard to understand, and those who are ignorant and unstable have twisted his letters to mean something quite different, just as they do with other parts of Scripture. And this will result in their destruction.

—2 PETER 3:3–16

Now the Holy Spirit tells us clearly that in the last times some will turn away from the true faith; they will follow deceptive spirits and teachings that come from demons. These people are hypocrites and liars, and their consciences are dead. They will say it is wrong to be married and wrong to eat certain foods. But God created those foods to be eaten with thanks by faithful people who know the truth. Since everything God created is good, we should not reject any of it but receive it with thanks. For we know it is made acceptable by the word of God and prayer.

—1 TIMOTHY 4:1–5

You should know this, Timothy, that in the last days there will be very difficult times. For people will love only themselves and their money. They will be boastful and proud, scoffing at God, disobedient to their parents, and ungrateful. They will consider nothing sacred. They will be unloving and unforgiving; they will slander others and have no self-control. They will be cruel and hate what is good. They will betray their friends, be reckless, be puffed up with pride, and love pleasure rather than God. They will act religious, but they will reject the power that could make them godly. Stay away from people like that!

—2 TIMOTHY 3:1–5

Enoch, who lived in the seventh generation after Adam, prophesied about these people. He said, "Listen! The Lord is coming with countless thousands of his holy ones to execute judgment on the people of the world. He will convict every person of all the ungodly things they have done and for all the insults that ungodly sinners have spoken against him." These people are grumblers and complainers, living only to satisfy their desires. They brag loudly about themselves, and they flatter others to get what they want.

But you, my dear friends, must remember what the apostles of our Lord Jesus Christ said. They told you that in the last times there would be scoffers whose purpose in life is to satisfy their ungodly desires. These people are the ones who are creating divisions among you. They follow their natural instincts because they do not have God's Spirit in them.

—JUDE 14–19

As the purpose of this book is to focus on what Jesus has to say about the end of the world from the Gospels and the Book of Revelation, I shall not comment much further in this chapter on what the apostles said other than to say again that it is evident that they believed what Jesus had taught them. In turn, they instructed the believers that the end of the world will be a reality at an appointed time, and that they needed to live their lives in readiness in order to enter the kingdom of heaven, whether the end came in their lifetime or not.

The apostles, who are our very first brothers in Christ, who lived and moved in the presence of Jesus for three years while He taught them about the kingdom of heaven and how to live, have written letters for all believers to read, study, understand and apply. Their letters not only taught the early believers but are also teaching us today. In the scriptures I have listed, they are teaching us about the signs of the end times and the end of the world. They are teaching it as fact, effectively saying, "This is what will happen."

In the current times we are living in, which bear the escalating marks of many of the end-time signs of which Jesus has warned us, we really do need to wake up and seriously take on board what the apostles are telling us. Every day that passes is a day nearer to Jesus' return. Come on, church, wake yourselves up and shake yourselves out of the heavy slumber that has come upon you through listening to too much comforting but deceiving doctrine that is not in keeping with the entirety of the Word of God. Listen to the painful truth that God speaks to you out of His heart of love for you. God does *not* warn us of judgment and hell because He hates us; God warns believers and unbelievers alike about judgment and hell because He *loves* us and wants us *all* to come to repentance and turn to Jesus to save us. God's stern warnings are His grace, His love and His mercy towards us. But many believers consider God's warnings as a hindrance to their lives, and something that they can just conveniently discard as irrelevant. Woe be unto us when we do this!

> Be careful that you do not refuse to listen to the One who is speaking. For if the people of Israel did not escape when they refused to listen to Moses, the earthly messenger, we will certainly not escape if we reject the One who speaks to us from heaven!
>
> —HEBREWS 12:25

Instead, let us give thanks to God for the faithful reporting of the end-time events by the apostles. They are given to us like warning lights on a car dashboard. We are to watch out for them as warnings of impending disaster ahead. They are warning signs for us to attend to what needs dealing with in our lives and to put matters right in accordance with our spiritual "maintenance manual," the Holy Bible.

Without Jesus warning us to be watchful and ready for the end times, and without the apostles reinforcing what Jesus has said about it through their teaching to the disciples, we would not be able to discern when Jesus' return is "at the door" (Mark 13:29; see also Matthew 24:32). Perhaps it is time we took this matter very seriously, with humble and thankful hearts that our first brothers in Christ were faithful and obedient to Jesus in continuing to teach this vital and now extremely urgent message.

Somehow over the last few decades, the importance of preaching and teaching the end-time message of Jesus' return and the end of the world has almost disappeared from the pulpits of our churches. This is catastrophic! And the end result of this neglect will be even more catastrophic! As those who profess to be followers of Christ, we cannot afford to dismiss, ignore, and neglect this most vital matter, which Jesus commanded us to be alert to and watchful and ready for.

Come on, church! Wake up! We need to do something about it—now.

Chapter 5
WHAT THE PROPHETS SAID

IRSTLY, LET'S ASK ourselves this question: what is a prophet of the Lord, and what is the prophet's purpose? A prophet of the Lord is a person (male or female, but for the purpose of the next few paragraphs I will refer to the prophet as "him") who speaks forth the Word of God and the warnings of God, regardless of how His Word may be received by all who hear or read it. To the prophet, obeying the Lord's requirement to speak forth His Word and His warnings is vital; it is without question. The prophet feels the great compelling hand of the Holy Spirit upon him urging him to speak, even though he may be ignored, ridiculed, and rejected as a doom monger and a fanatic.

A thorough read through the Old Testament will reveal that this was the case for the majority of the Old Testament prophets. It is still the same today. The prophets of the Lord did not become extinct at Jesus' first coming. Obedient prophets of the Lord have been needed throughout the past two millennia and are even more urgently needed in these times in which we are living.

The prophets of the Lord will be speaking forth the Word of God and the warnings of God right up until the final trumpet shall sound, at Jesus' Second Coming. Anyone who, like the prophet Isaiah, hears the call of the Lord and responds by saying, "Here am I. Send me!" (Isa. 6:8, NIV), can be considered to be a prophet of the Lord regardless of what high or low position he or she may hold in this life on earth or in their church. The Lord often uses the most weak, weary, and insignificant of human beings to speak His warnings in order to demonstrate that it is His power that

is working in and through them. We do not have to be a natu-
rally gifted or trained public speaker to be used by God to speak
His message. We just need to have willing and obedient hearts
to do what God is compelling us to do through the power of the
Holy Spirit. The apostle Paul confirms this in his first letter to the
Corinthian church:

> When I first came to you, dear brothers and sisters, I didn't
> use lofty words and impressive wisdom to tell you God's
> secret plan. For I decided that while I was with you I would
> forget everything except Jesus Christ, the One who was cru-
> cified. I came to you in weakness—timid and trembling. And
> my message and my preaching were very plain. Rather than
> using clever and persuasive speeches, I relied only on the
> power of the Holy Spirit. I did this so you would trust not in
> human wisdom but in the power of God.
>
> —1 CORINTHIANS 2:1–5

> Remember, dear brothers and sisters, that few of you were
> wise in the world's eyes or powerful or wealthy when God
> called you. Instead, God chose things the world considers
> foolish in order to shame those who think they are wise.
> And he chose things that are powerless to shame those who
> are powerful. God chose things despised by the world, things
> counted as nothing at all, and used them to bring to nothing
> what the world considers important.
>
> —1 CORINTHIANS 1:26–28

I urge you, dear reader, if you have heard the voice of the
Lord compelling you to speak forth His Word and His warnings
without compromise, obey Him regardless of the obstacles others
may throw in your path to prevent you from speaking. Do not
put it off any longer. God wants to use you to fulfill His eternal
purposes. The part God wants you to fulfill is vital to His end-
time plans. Your part may be small and you may wonder what

difference it would make whether you fulfill it or not, but your part may be the catalyst that creates a situation that could bring a million people to salvation through hearing the gospel message of Jesus Christ. But if you do not fulfill the part He is compelling you to do, those million people may never come to salvation. When God speaks to us and we fail to obey Him, our disobedience could reap devastating eternal consequences for millions of people. This is an extremely sobering thought.

A prophet of the Lord has to accept the reality of the rejection and mockery he is likely to face from the unbelieving world and also from those within the house of God. "The prophet is a watchman. . . . He faces hostility even in the house of God" (Hosea 9:8). The heart's desire of the prophet is to obey and honor the Lord who has given to him the message he must speak. He is to seek praises only from God, not the praises of man.

Now that we have established the purpose of a prophet of the Lord, let's begin our look at what the Old Testament prophets spoke concerning the end times that the Lord inspired them to speak through the power of the Holy Spirit. What they spoke and prophesied is not irrelevant to us today. Much Old Testament prophecy was specific to those actual times, but there is also a great deal of prophecy that clearly did not relate to the times they were living in.

These end-time prophecies recorded in the Bible by the Old Testament prophets were intended by the Lord to be recognized and understood *only* by those who would become the generation that will "not pass away until all these have happened" (Matt. 24:34, NIV; Mark 13:30, NIV; Luke 21:32, NIV).

In recent years, Old Testament prophecies have been and are being fulfilled at a phenomenal rate, although many believers are not aware of it simply because they are not opening their eyes to the fact or do not wish to be disturbed out of their daily routine. However, media technology is awash with evidence that may fit end-time Bible prophecy fulfillment, despite our ignorance of it.

It would seem that the Lord has given us the means to be able to find out for ourselves very easily and very quickly what is happening around the world in order to discern whether these fit the description of end-time Bible prophecy.

In the Book of Daniel, twice the prophet was told by the angel to seal up the prophetic visions that he was shown "until the time of the end" (Dan. 12:4) and "until the appointed time of the end" (8:19, NIV). This would seem to indicate that at the time of the end, the meanings and the fulfillments of the end-time prophecies that Daniel was given would become unsealed and made available for discernment to the generation that will "not pass away until all these things have happened" (Matt. 24:34, NIV; Mark 13:30, NIV; Luke 21:32, NIV).

Could we be the generation Jesus is talking about? Up until the invention and rapid progression of computer technology over the past few decades, it was not really possible to rapidly collect so much data relating to world events and spread its evidence around the globe at the touch of a few buttons. No period in history has had this ability. The end-time prophecies have remained sealed "until the time of the end" (Dan. 12:4). But we are in the era of being able to gather information in vast quantities, observing and discerning the evidence from the comfort of our armchairs. Are we in the era that the angel in Daniel's vision referred to? Have the prophecies in the Book of Daniel now become unsealed while the church has been in a serious state of slumber?

Many believers dismiss searching for these things on the Internet as nonsense and stupidity. But I disagree. I accept that there are scams which we must be wary of, but this is where the spiritual gift of discernment should be readily used. What is the point of possessing the gift of discernment if we don't then use it?

By and large, many of the online articles are actually news reports showing what is happening around the world on an ever increasing and often unprecedented scale. There is a vast amount of evidence that is accumulating before our eyes, often posted by people who are determined to uncover and report the truth often left out of the mainstream news.

Bible prophecy in both the Old and New Testament is being fulfilled in our lifetime. But Satan does not want the world to know about this because he knows that unbelievers might actually wake up and turn to Jesus, thus being saved from eternity in hell. It would appear that Satan will resort to any means to keep end-time prophecy fulfillment hidden from the world's eyes and even from the eyes of Christians so that they will not be alert, watchful, and ready for when Jesus returns.

But there are courageous people out there who are determined to reveal the truth, using the Internet to report their findings often at great risk. Let's not dismiss all these things as nonsense posted by a bunch of fanatics. By studying Scripture we will be able to discern which reports are false and which ones actually confirm the Word of God and the fulfillment of Bible prophecy. There is a scripture saying that he who judges a matter before he has heard the whole story is a fool. The New Living Translation puts it this way: "Spouting off before listening to the facts is both shameful and foolish" (Prov. 18:13).

So, let us not cast sweeping assumptions and judgments upon evidence that may be presented to us until we have listened to all the evidence. At that point we can prayerfully weigh the matter up as to whether it is a confirmation of God's Word or a lie. The Holy Spirit will show us. I believe we ought to pay attention to some of the things that are posted on the Internet, as this may be the only means that some brave people have of reporting events that would appear to fit in with end-time Bible prophecy fulfillment.

Let's turn it the other way around. Let's say that *we* are the ones who discovered something that seemed to fit the fulfillment of Bible prophecy and we desperately wanted to make it known to inform other believers and to warn unbelievers. If we tried to report it to our local or mainstream media, it is highly likely that we would be ridiculed and would probably be asked to leave the building. If that were the case, our only resort would be to post our findings on the Internet; and we would really hope that others would want to read or watch our report, believe what we are saying, and share it with others.

Let us be courageous enough to search out what is really happening in the world today that could possibly be a fulfillment of Bible prophecy, and not just assume that the edited information we hear on the mainstream news is the total sum of the matter. We might find ourselves in for a shock at what we discover and where we may be in relation to the last days.

So, let's begin our look at what some of the Old Testament prophets had to say about the end of the world. While there are many long and detailed prophecies that could be listed in this chapter, I am only selecting a few just to confirm that the end of the world was prophesied during Old Testament times, which is in line with Jesus' teaching about it in the New Testament and the Book of Revelation.

The first long passage from Ezekiel 38 below is incredible when we see it in the light of the end-time vision that the apostle John was given by the angel of the Lord in Revelation 20:7–9, which reads,

> When the thousand years are over, Satan will be released from his prison and will go out to deceive the nations in the four corners of the earth—Gog and Magog—and to gather them for battle. In number they are like the sand on the seashore. They marched across the breadth of the earth and surrounded the camp of God's people, the city he loves. But fire came down from heaven and devoured them.
> —REVELATION 20:7–9, NIV

The following is the Word of the Lord given to the Old Testament prophet Ezekiel. This describes in more detail the end-time event revealed to the apostle John, recorded in Revelation 20:7–9.

This is another message that came to me from the LORD: "Son of man, turn and face Gog of the land of Magog, the prince who rules over the nations of Meshech and Tubal, and prophesy against him. Give him this message from the Sovereign LORD: Gog, I am your enemy! I will turn you around and put hooks in your jaws to lead you out with your whole army—your horses and charioteers in full armor and a great horde armed with shields and swords. Persia, Ethiopia, and Libya will join you, too, with all their weapons. Gomer and all its armies will also join you, along with the armies of Beth-togarmah from the distant north, and many others.

"Get ready; be prepared! Keep all the armies around you mobilized, and take command of them. A long time from now you will be called into action. In the distant future you will swoop down on the land of Israel, which will be enjoying peace after recovering from war and after its people have returned from many lands to the mountains of Israel. You and all your allies—a vast and awesome army—will roll down on them like a storm and cover the land like a cloud.

"This is what the Sovereign LORD says: At that time evil thoughts will come to your mind, and you will devise a wicked scheme. You will say, 'Israel is an unprotected land filled with unwalled villages! I will march against her and destroy these people who live in such confidence! I will go to those formerly desolate cities that are now filled with people who have returned from exile in many nations. I will capture vast amounts of plunder, for the people are rich with livestock and other possessions now. They think the whole world revolves around them!' But Sheba and Dedan and the merchants of Tarshish will ask, 'Do you really think the armies you have gathered can rob them of silver and gold? Do you think you can drive away their livestock and seize their goods and carry off plunder?'

"Therefore, son of man, prophesy against Gog. Give him this message from the Sovereign LORD: When my people are living in peace in their land, then you will rouse yourself.

You will come from your homeland in the distant north with your vast cavalry and your mighty army, and you will attack my people Israel, covering their land like a cloud. At that time in the distant future, I will bring you against my land as everyone watches, and my holiness will be displayed by what happens to you, Gog. Then all the nations will know that I am the LORD.

"This is what the Sovereign LORD asks: Are you the one I was talking about long ago, when I announced through Israel's prophets that in the future I would bring you against my people? But this is what the Sovereign LORD says: When Gog invades the land of Israel, my fury will boil over! In my jealousy and blazing anger, I promise a mighty shaking in the land of Israel on that day. All living things—the fish in the sea, the birds of the sky, the animals of the field, the small animals that scurry along the ground, and all the people on earth—will quake in terror at my presence. Mountains will be thrown down; cliffs will crumble; walls will fall to the earth. I will summon the sword against you on all the hills of Israel, says the Sovereign LORD. Your men will turn their swords against each other. I will punish you and your armies with disease and bloodshed; I will send torrential rain, hailstones, fire, and burning sulfur! In this way, I will show my greatness and holiness, and I will make myself known to all the nations of the world. Then they will know that I am the LORD."

—EZEKIEL 38:1–23

At that time Michael, the archangel who stands guard over your nation, will arise. Then there will be a time of anguish greater than any since nations first came into existence. But at that time every one of your people whose name is written in the book will be rescued. Many of those whose bodies lie dead and buried will rise up, some to everlasting life and some to shame and everlasting disgrace.

—DANIEL 12:1–2

The LORD of Heaven's Armies says, "The day of judgment is coming, burning like a furnace. On that day the arrogant and the wicked will be burned up like straw. They will be consumed—roots, branches, and all."

—MALACHI 4:1

"That terrible day of the LORD is near. Swiftly it comes—a day of bitter tears, a day when even strong men will cry out. It will be a day when the Lord's anger is poured out—a day of terrible distress and anguish, a day of ruin and desolation, a day of darkness and gloom, a day of clouds and blackness, a day of trumpet calls and battle cries. Down go the walled cities and the strongest battlements! Because you have sinned against the LORD, I will make you grope around like the blind. Your blood will be poured into the dust, and your bodies will lie rotting on the ground."

Your silver and gold will not save you on that day of the LORD's anger. For the whole land will be devoured by the fire of his jealousy. He will make a terrifying end of all the people on earth.

—ZEPHANIAH 1:14–18

Gather together—yes, gather together, you shameless nation. Gather before judgment begins, before your time to repent is blown away like chaff. Act now, before the fierce fury of the LORD falls and the terrible day of the LORD's anger begins.

—ZEPHANIAH 2:1–2

Dress yourselves in burlap and weep, you priests! Wail, you who serve before the altar! Come, spend the night in burlap, you ministers of my God. For there is no grain or wine to offer at the Temple of your God. Announce a time of fasting; call the people together for a solemn meeting. Bring the leaders and all the people of the land into the Temple of the LORD your God, and cry out to him there. The day of the LORD is near, the day when destruction comes from the Almighty. How terrible that day will be!

Our food disappears before our very eyes. No joyful celebrations are held in the house of our God. The seeds die in the parched ground, and the grain crops fail. The barns stand empty, and granaries are abandoned. How the animals moan with hunger! The herds of cattle wander about confused, because they have no pasture. The flocks of sheep and goats bleat in misery.

LORD, help us! The fire has consumed the wilderness pastures, and flames have burned up all the trees. Even the wild animals cry out to you because the streams have dried up, and fire has consumed the wilderness pastures.

—JOEL 1:13–20

Sound the alarm in Jerusalem! Raise the battle cry on my holy mountain! Let everyone tremble in fear because the day of the LORD is upon us. It is a day of darkness and gloom, a day of thick clouds and deep blackness. Suddenly, like dawn spreading across the mountains, a great and mighty army appears. Nothing like it has been seen before or will ever be seen again. Fire burns in front of them, and flames follow after them. Ahead of them the land lies as beautiful as the Garden of Eden. Behind them is nothing but desolation; not one thing escapes. They look like horses; they charge forward like warhorses. Look at them as they leap along the mountaintops. Listen to the noise they make—like the rumbling of chariots, like the roar of fire sweeping across a field of stubble, or like a mighty army moving into battle.

Fear grips all the people; every face grows pale with terror. The attackers march like warriors and scale city walls like soldiers. Straight forward they march, never breaking rank. They never jostle each other; each moves in exactly the right position. They break through defenses without missing a step. They swarm over the city and run along its walls. They enter all the houses, climbing like thieves through the windows.

The earth quakes as they advance, and the heavens tremble. The sun and moon grow dark, and the stars no longer shine.

The Lord is at the head of the column. He leads them with a shout. This is his mighty army, and they follow his orders. The day of the Lord is an awesome, terrible thing. Who can possibly survive?

—Joel 2:1–11

Then, after doing all those things, I will pour out my Spirit upon all people. Your sons and daughters will prophesy. Your old men will dream dreams, and your young men will see visions. In those days I will pour out my Spirit even on servants—men and women alike. And I will cause wonders in the heavens and on the earth—blood and fire and columns of smoke. The sun will become dark, and the moon will turn blood red before that great and terrible day of the Lord arrives.

—Joel 2:28–31

"Let the nations be called to arms. Let them march to the valley of Jehoshaphat. There I, the Lord, will sit to pronounce judgment on them all. Swing the sickle, for the harvest is ripe. Come, tread the grapes, for the winepress is full. The storage vats are overflowing with the wickedness of these people."

Thousands upon thousands are waiting in the valley of decision. There the day of the Lord will soon arrive. The sun and moon will grow dark, and the stars will no longer shine. The Lord's voice will roar from Zion and thunder from Jerusalem, and the heavens and the earth will shake. But the Lord will be a refuge for his people, a strong fortress for the people of Israel.

—Joel 3:12–16

For further detailed reading, prayerful study and seeking the Lord for wisdom and discernment, I would suggest reading Daniel chapters 7 and 8. Daniel is told to "seal up the vision, for it concerns the distant future" (8:26, NIV). In Daniel 8:19 he is told that the vision concerns the "appointed time of the end" (NIV). I encourage you to also read Daniel chapters 11 and 12 where again Daniel is told that the visions are for the time of the end, and that the words are closed up and sealed until this time. It would be beneficial to read the visions and prophecies in the Book of Daniel in the light of the end-time events in the Book of Revelation chapters 4 through 22.

It is important to remember the fact that the prophecies in the Book of Daniel have been sealed up since the time they were given to him in these visions: sealed up *until* the time of the end. At the "appointed time," these prophecies *will* be opened and fulfilled upon the earth. As I mentioned in chapter 3, the apostle John is also shown the vision of the end-time events; but he is told *not* to seal up the vision, which would indicate that the prophecies concerning the end of the world were sealed from the time of Daniel's vision *until* the time of the apostle John's vision. Therefore, from that time on the prophetic visions of the end of the world became *unsealed*, as the angel told the apostle John *not* to seal them up again. If these prophecies are no longer sealed and have in fact been open since that time, it would seem that all that remains is for their complete fulfillment. This should be a very sobering thought to anyone who professes to be a believer.

The visions in the Book of Daniel refer to beasts, rams, goats, heads, and horns; and it is easy to become confused as to what it all means. As I mentioned in chapter 3, I believe they refer to kingdoms, nations, leaders of nations, and to political organizations, and religious organizations that would appear to be pretending to represent Christianity but are in fact wolves in sheep's clothing—false prophets, false teachers, and even false messiahs. This is why the Lord exhorts believers to be alert and watchful and discern what is happening in the world, as not all that we see is actually the truth. Much religious activity, even that which is portrayed in the name of Christianity, may be a deception dressed up to look like the truth.

As these prophecies were given in Old Testament times to God's prophets and are confirmed by Jesus in the New Testament, we can be sure that they will come to pass upon the earth. God says that His Word does not return to Him void. It will accomplish His purpose (Isa. 55:11, KJV).

As believers, how can we possibly continue to ignore the consistent warnings by the prophets, the apostles, and Jesus Himself to heed the truth and the reality that the world will come to an end at an appointed time? How can we continue to ignore Jesus' instruction to do our part by being alert and watchful and living our Christian lives in readiness for His appearing? How will we know when Jesus' return is "at the door" if we go about our daily lives with no thought or concern whatsoever about it?

All of heaven is aware of the unfolding fulfillment of Bible prophecy, as it escalates towards the great Day of the Lord. But the generation to whom the end-time prophecies appear to relate seems oblivious to it all. The bride of Christ has never been so sleepy. As believers if we remain in this slumber, it is highly likely that our halfhearted and complacent attitude towards the return of the Bridegroom could result in the doors to the marriage of the Lamb and His bride being shut in our faces. We will be calling to Jesus, saying, "Lord! Lord! Open the door for us!" (Matt. 25:11). And He will reply, "Believe me, I do not know you!" (v. 12).

We urgently need to live our lives on earth in obedience to the Word of God so that we never have to hear such devastating words from Jesus on the day that He returns to redeem His pure and spotless bride. We really do not want to end up being like one of the five unwise virgins who failed to keep themselves ready for the Bridegroom's return and ended up being left outside the door, with the Bridegroom stating that he never knew them. (See Matthew 25:10–12.)

Stephanie Cottam says,

> We, as the Bride of Christ, are called to be ready. And as we
> see in the parable of the ten virgins, there is a stark warning
> that if we are not ready, we will miss the wedding—and once
> the doors are shut, they are shut![1]

Let's stop kidding ourselves that our unconfessed and unrepentant sins don't matter to God! The scriptures consistently prove that they *do* matter to God and that eternal torment in hell is very likely to be the consequence if we do not confess and repent of them urgently. How much longer are we going to play games with our salvation? Let's stop being foolish. God cannot be mocked. What we sow we will reap (Gal. 6:7). We need to fear the One who is able to destroy both body *and* soul in hell (Matt. 10:28).

When Jesus returns He will separate the sheep from the goats. The sheep will receive eternal life in heaven and the goats will go to eternal torment in hell. At the final end of the world, all evil will be cast into the lake of fire along with Satan and his demons. This is the final place of eternal torment, where the flames and the smoke of the eternal torment will never be extinguished. Eternity is forever. It is endless and unceasing. Therefore eternal torment in hell will *never* end. Most of us cannot even bear any sort of torment on earth for a single day. So what causes us to dismiss the truth of the horrifying reality of eternity in hell that God warns us to diligently avoid through the clear and graphic description of it in His Word? Why do we allow our minds to casually dismiss it as nothing to worry about? How can we continue living our Christian lives in such a way that could cause us to be at risk of spending eternity in the lake of fire, and this be nothing to worry about?

God's prophets have warned us that the end of the world and the consequences it will bring *will* come. Many of the prophets were ridiculed, persecuted, and even put to death for fulfilling the call of God upon their lives. They boldly spoke of God's justice and wrath that will come at the end upon all who are disobedient, rebellious, and unbelieving.

> Now go and write down these words. Write them in a book. They will stand until the end of time as a witness that these people are stubborn rebels who refuse to pay attention to the LORD's instructions. They tell the seers, "Stop seeing visions!" They tell the prophets, "Don't tell us what is right. Tell us nice things. Tell us lies. Forget all this gloom. Get off your narrow path. Stop telling us about your 'Holy One of Israel.'"
> —ISAIAH 30:8–11

Throughout history, mankind has continued to ignore the warnings of God, which He has spoken through whomever He has chosen to use. This is still the case in the world today, and even many in the church at this present time are still ignoring the warnings of prophecy. This very fact is recorded in the Old Testament, as we saw earlier in this chapter: "The prophet is a watchman.... He faces hostility even in the house of God" (Hosea 9:8). When the end of the world finally comes, we cannot blame God if we find ourselves in the place of eternal torment, where we complacently and pridefully thought we would never end up.

Let us finish this chapter by thanking the Lord for these Old Testament prophets who took seriously the warnings of God, obediently spoke His message, endured the mockery of those who opposed His message, and even lost their lives for their faithfulness to the Lord.

Chapter 6
THE END OF THE WORLD FOR BELIEVERS

But God's truth stands firm like a foundation stone with this inscription: "The LORD knows those who are his," and "All who belong to the LORD must turn away from evil."
—2 TIMOTHY 2:19

The night is almost gone; the day of salvation will soon be here. So remove your dark deeds like dirty clothes, and put on the shining armor of right living.
—ROMANS 13:12

Having therefore these promises, dearly beloved, let us cleanse ourselves from all filthiness of the flesh and spirit, perfecting holiness in the fear of God.
—2 CORINTHIANS 7:1, KJV

Above all, you must live as citizens of heaven, conducting your-selves in a manner worthy of the Good News about Christ.
—PHILIPPIANS 1:27A

IT IS MY joy to write this chapter because it will reveal the glory of the wonderful inheritance and the blessings that are laid up in heaven for all those who are true believers.

But first of all, let us examine what it means to be a true believer for whom eternal life in the kingdom of heaven is promised. Jesus said that we would know who believers are by their fruit (Matt. 7:16, 20)—not just the fruit of the Spirit listed in Galatians 5:22–23, but the fruit that is demonstrated in our daily lives by obedient application of the Word of God. The life of a true believer should outwardly express his or her belief and obedience to the Word of God. If we do not "practice what we preach," then Jesus says we are hypocrites, whitewashed tombs full of filth and dead men's bones (Matt. 23:27).

Secondly, we need to examine our right to declare ourselves to be a true child of God based solely on the christening or baptism we may have received as an infant. I humbly ask if you would be able to bear with me on this delicate subject, because I know that it is a very sensitive area for many people. I would like to reassure you that I am writing this from my own personal experience—my own baptism as an infant many years ago in 1961 and the things the Lord has shown me since He opened my eyes to His Word so that I could see, understand, and obey.

Many churches call this ceremony infant baptism or christening. Irrespective of what it is called, after the ceremony has been undertaken, the infant's name is put into the parish register as someone who has been baptized into the "family of God." A certificate of baptism is then given. Even if we never actually go to church, many of us who have been baptized as an infant will fill in forms that ask what faith we belong to by writing the word *Christian* in the box or we may enter the denomination that we were baptized into, such as *Anglican* or *Methodist*. However, as we know from God's Word, fulfilling religious rituals that have been handed down for generations do not make a person a child of God.

While I appreciate that the context of the following passage was in relation to the disciples not washing their hands before eating, nevertheless, Jesus' reply can be applied to all religious traditions that are practiced, adhered to, and affirmed as fulfilling scripture, when in fact scripture is telling us that our religious traditions are contrary to the commandments of God.

> Some Pharisees and teachers of religious law now arrived from Jerusalem to see Jesus. They asked him, "Why do your disciples disobey our age-old tradition?...Jesus replied, "And why do you, by your traditions, violate the direct commandments of God?"
>
> —Matthew 15:1–3

Further,

> This people draweth nigh unto me with their mouth, and honoureth me with their lips; but their heart is far from me. But in vain they do worship me, teaching for doctrines the commandments of men.
>
> —Matthew 15:8–9, kjv

Yes, the Word of God does say that we are all created in God's image (Gen. 1:27). In fact, the whole of the human race is created "in the image of God," but this fact does not mean that we are actual sons or daughters of God. Something has got to happen in us in order for us to go from simply being created in His image to actually becoming a son or daughter of God. This happens when we believe that Jesus Christ is who He says He is—the Son of God, the Messiah, our Lord and Savior. Once we truly believe this, we need to pray for the Holy Spirit to bring us to that crushing place of conviction of our sins, then we need to confess and repent of them and turn to Jesus Christ to save us.

When we have made that spiritual transaction and accept, believe in, and trust in the sacrifice that took place on the cross to open up the way for all mankind to approach God's throne of mercy and grace in order to be forgiven, cleansed, healed, and reconciled to God; *when we put our faith in Jesus Christ as our Lord and Savior; only then* do we become born again from above and become a child of God.

The apostle John writes,

He came to that which was his own, but his own did not receive him. *Yet to all who did receive him, to those who believed in his name, he gave the right to become children of God*—children born not of natural descent, nor of human decision or a husband's will, but born of God.

—John 1:11–13, NIV, EMPHASIS ADDED

So, to declare that we are a child of God based solely on the fact that we have been baptized as an infant and have a certificate of baptism from the parish register to prove it is not enough to confirm our right to call ourselves a child of God.

Ryle, who was the first Anglican bishop of Liverpool in 1880, puts it very sternly,

Tell me not that you have been baptized, and taught the Catechism of the Church of England, and therefore must be a child of God. I tell you that the parish register is not the Book of Life.[1]

Very strong words indeed! I have not written the above to make anyone feel condemned if they have not yet been baptized by full immersion as an adult believer. I myself was baptized as an infant and felt that I didn't need to be baptized by full immersion as an adult until someone showed me in the Bible that Jesus had been baptized in the River Jordan. He is our example.

Then Jesus went from Galilee to the Jordan River to be baptized by John. But John tried to talk him out of it. "I am the one who needs to be baptized by you," he said, "so why are you coming to me?" But Jesus said, "It should be done, for we must carry out all that God requires." So John agreed to baptize him.

—Matthew 3:13–15

This passage of scripture is so amazing that it is able to stand on its own as the only scripture necessary to convict us of the need for full immersion baptism as a believer. Even John the Baptist is exclaiming to Jesus that he needs Jesus to baptize him, not the other way around.

But as it is always good to find other scriptures when seeking confirmation on a matter, I also discovered two other very specific examples where some people were baptized immediately. In fact, in the situation at Cornelius' house, the apostle Peter *ordered* those who had just received the Holy Spirit, to be baptized. In the other situation, the Ethiopian eunuch virtually *demanded* to be baptized. Let's have a look at these two passages.

> While Peter was still speaking these words, the Holy Spirit came on all who heard the message. The circumcised believers who had come with Peter were astonished that the gift of the Holy Spirit had been poured out even on Gentiles. For they heard them speaking in tongues and praising God. Then Peter said, *"Surely no one can stand in the way of their being baptized with water. They have received the Holy Spirit just as we have." So he ordered that they be baptized in the name of Jesus Christ.*
> —ACTS 10:44–48, NIV, EMPHASIS ADDED

> Then Philip began with that very passage of Scripture and told him the good news about Jesus. As they traveled along the road, they came to some water *and the eunuch said, "Look, here is water. What can stand in the way of my being baptized?" And he gave orders to stop the chariot. Then both Philip and the eunuch went down into the water and Philip baptized him.*
> —ACTS 8:35–38, NIV, EMPHASIS ADDED

I find these two accounts extremely humbling. In both situations it is clear that full immersion baptism was not an optional extra. The urgency in both situations is irrefutable evidence that baptism in this manner was absolutely essential and not to be delayed. Do we have this same attitude towards full immersion baptism, or do we debate its necessity because of our own personal thoughts and opinion?

In his second letter to the Corinthian church, the apostle Paul writes,

> Casting down arguments and every high thing that exalts itself against the knowledge of God, bringing every thought into captivity to the obedience of Christ,"
> —2 CORINTHIANS 10:5, NKJV

As followers of Christ, we need to cast down every thought and opinion we hold tightly to that is diametrically opposed to the Word of God. We then need to bring our thoughts and opinions into captivity so that they come into obedience to what God's Word requires of us. When Jesus clearly teaches us that we need to be baptized by full immersion and other scriptures confirm and uphold this, if our thoughts and opinions resist and resent what God's Word teaches, then we are the ones who are in error. We must quickly repent of our rebellion and bring every thought into obedience to Christ and then do what He commands.

Do our churches have a sense of urgency about baptism? If our church has a baptism pool, is it filled up every week in expectation that the Holy Spirit will cause people in the pews to come forward and demand that they be baptized immediately? As churches, are we ready for this or do we only have set times for baptism services, perhaps twice a year? Does our church calendar make way for the sudden outpouring of the Holy Spirit, causing people to demand to be baptized? These are serious questions that we need to ask ourselves and do something about if we find that we are falling short of obedience to God's holy Word on this vital matter. Jesus Himself says, "*Follow me* and be my disciple" (Matt. 9:9, emphasis added). He also says, "*My sheep listen to my voice*; I know them, and *they follow me*" (John 10:27, emphasis added).

Notice in the second passage above Jesus says His sheep listen to His voice, and that they follow Him. If Jesus says that to be His disciple we must "follow Him," then we must follow Him in every sense of the word. The Word of God on the issue of baptism is all that is needed to convict us of the vital need to be baptized in the same way that Jesus was baptized. We must come to the place where we follow His example out of obedience to His Word and because of our love for Him. If we find that our heart is constantly struggling with this issue, I deeply believe that following Jesus in the example of baptism will bring us the peace that we long for. It is obedience that Jesus requires of His disciples. I pray that what I have written on this sensitive matter will enable you to feel God's love for you and the blessings He wishes to bestow upon you through your obedience.

So let's now continue to have a look at some things that the Word of God says will be the evidence of a true believer. Stating it simply, a true follower of Christ believes what God says in His Word, desires to live their life according to it, and diligently endeavors to do so.

I accept that there will be some who may take exception to some of the things I will list, aside from the issue of baptism; but nevertheless, if God's Word says it then that is what counts. If we dismiss what we don't like or don't agree with, then that should cause us to ask ourselves whether we are rebelling against the authority of God's Word. If this is the case, we ought then to examine our heart, our mind, and our life; question whether we are a true believer; and then do something to rectify our rebellion. A true believer would be someone who:

1. Believes that Jesus Christ is the Son of God, who was crucified on the cross and took upon Himself the weight and punishment of the sins of the whole world in order to open up the way for all mankind to receive eternal life and enter the kingdom of heaven *when* they confess and repent of their sins

and put their faith in Jesus as their Lord and Savior and become born again (see John 3:3–7).

2. Acknowledges the truth that they will still occasionally sin even as a Christian; but understands that they need to confess these things to God and to those they have sinned against and to repent of them (see 1 John 1:8–10).

3. Accepts the truth that Jesus was baptized in order to show us that we need to follow His example out of obedience, and to be baptized in the same manner as He was, to fulfill scripture (see Matthew 3:13–15). As I have already written on this matter, I will not say much more other than that God's Word also says that a servant is not greater than his master (Matt. 10:24). So if we resist full immersion baptism when our Master (Jesus) has demonstrated that we need to do this, then we need to repent of our rebellion and quickly put the matter right by making a commitment to God to obey His Word on this issue. Jesus is the Master, we are His servant. The servant obeys the Master.

4. Is filled with the Holy Spirit in accordance with the scriptures (see Mark 16:15–18; Acts 2:1–4; 10:46).

5. Has the ability to operate in the use of the spiritual gifts in the church, as the Lord directs them (see 1 Corinthians 14).

6. Feeds on the Word of God as their daily bread with study and prayer, and desires to live their life in obedience to it (see 2 Timothy 2:15; Psalm 1:1–2). They respond quickly in repentance to the conviction that the Lord brings when they have strayed from

God's Word or are considering straying from it (see Revelation 3:19).

7. Apologizes to those concerned when they have made mistakes, offended them, caused hurt or harm, or sinned in any way; puts the matter right and does not make excuses for their actions by saying, "God forgives me, so that's all that matters." Yes, it is true that God forgives us of our sin when we confess it to Him (1 John 1:9), but the Lord also requires us to go to the one we have sinned against and apologize to them, seek their forgiveness, and put our relationship with them right again (see Matthew 5:23–24).

We should *not* proudly comfort ourselves with the fact that God's Word says He has forgiven us when the person we have sinned against and caused hurt to is still distressed because we are too proud to go to them to admit and confess that we have sinned against them. We are often too proud to ask for their forgiveness but we still want and even expect God to forgive us. Many use God's forgiveness of our sins as a shortcut, when in fact we should be obediently following all that His Word says on the matter. God will not give us the peace of His forgiveness until we have put right with others the wrong we have done to them (see Matthew 5:23–24).

The same applies if we are holding onto unforgiveness towards someone who has sinned against us. If they won't come to us to admit it, scripture instructs us that we are to go and tell them what it is that they have done so that the Holy Spirit can convict them of their sin in order that we can also forgive them (see Matthew 18:15). But if we don't do this, we give the devil a foothold in our lives, causing us to dwell on our wounds. This then causes unforgiveness to take root. There is a godly order to this and true believers will trust in God's Word and follow it.

8. Demonstrates Christlike sacrificial love, not only to fellow brothers and sisters in Christ, but also to their "enemies" (see Matthew 5:44; Luke 6:27–31, 35).

9. Tithes of their time, possessions, and finances in accordance with scripture (see Malachi 3:6–12; Matthew 23:23).

10. Does not show favoritism (see James 2:1–4, NIV).

11. Obeys God's commands (see John 14:15, NIV).

When we fail as a believer, we must not pretend that we haven't. We must confess it quickly, repent of it, and receive God's mercy, forgiveness, and cleansing. We must then move forward in faith that our relationship with God has been restored. We must not allow ourselves to wallow in Satan's condemnation of our failure. We need to get up out of our mess, agree with God about our sin, deal with it humbly before Him with a broken and contrite heart, and then put things right with those we have sinned against.

I am sure we have all experienced those who refuse to accept that they have done anything wrong despite the issue being clearly expressed to them; those who refuse to accept any responsibility for their own failings, who refuse to apologize for the hurt and damage their own failings have caused to others, yet still attend church and pretend that "all is well" by presenting a joyful façade while "all hell" is breaking loose and waging war inside them and around them.

This is a very serious issue in God's eyes for someone who says they are a believer. So serious is it that God's Word says that if we attend church while we are holding something against someone or if we have hurt someone but are not doing anything to put it right (i.e., pretending it doesn't exist or that it is trivial and doesn't matter), we are to leave our gift at the altar and go and put the matter right with the person we have hurt or who has hurt us (see Matthew 5:24). God is actually giving us permission not to attend church until we have done this vital thing. Attending church is about worshiping God, and we cannot do that sincerely and whole-heartedly if our hearts and minds are swamped with bitterness, resentment, hostility, hatred, and unforgiveness towards others.

> Whoever conceals their sins does not prosper, but the one who confesses and renounces them finds mercy.
> —PROVERBS 28:13, NIV

However, if you have truly done all that God requires you to do concerning conflict resolution but the other person still does not want to accept their failings or accept any responsibility for their part in causing a conflict, you must then leave them in God's hands. You are then free to return to the altar to worship God. You have done your part according to God's Word and so you can worship Him with a clear conscience.

12. Fellowships with other believers to encourage and support them and offer assistance to their needs and to listen to their struggles in order to offer help that is based on sound biblical doctrine (see Galatians 6:1–2) pointing them to God as the source and ultimate supplier of all their needs (Phil. 4:19).

13. Desires and wants to share the gospel with others (see 1 Peter 3:15).

14. Finally, a true believer is a person for whom saying *no* to the things of this world and *yes* to obedience to the Word of God is understood to be essential while we wait for Jesus' glorious appearing (see Titus 2:11–15); a person who has a deep conviction as to what exactly is at stake in the final outcome when Jesus returns and hastens in the end of the world (see Matthew 25:1–13).

All of the above I know to be true from the Word of God. There are many more things that could be listed here which demonstrate the evidence of a true follower of Jesus Christ, but I think we are able to get the picture of what it means from this list. A true believer is someone who is so thankful to God for what He has done through the Cross of Christ, to open up the way for us to be saved from the eternal penalty in hell for our sins, that they have a heart that is passionate towards the Lord and want to do the things that honor and please Him.

A true believer's heart should be repulsed at the memory of the sinful things they used to do; and, as such, their desire now is to crucify their flesh and all its selfish passions and cravings. A true believer desires to live their life "redeeming the time, because the days are evil" (Eph. 5:16, KJV), rather than being consumed by the craving to pursue the pleasures of the world.

The Holy Spirit is the One who makes everything that Jesus did for us real in our lives. But we must not have a casual attitude about our repetitive sinful behavior that says, "Yes, I know that I keep on messing up but I can't do anything about it. God will sort it all out for me." If we have this casual attitude about our sin, God will not just step in and make it all better for us. As believers, if we couldn't care less about our daily sins and have the attitude that expects God to do all the changing in us while we sit back and do nothing, we are truly deceiving ourselves.

God hears and responds to the prayers of those who admit their sins, confess their sins, repent of their sins, and ask Him to cleanse them, purify them, and transform them. The futility and destruction of our repetitive sins should drive us to the point where we come before God in brokenness over the state of our lives. When we are at this point, we know without a doubt that we cannot be changed without the power of the Holy Spirit working in our lives. The Holy Spirit cannot dwell in the same place where sin dwells, whether that is in us as an individual or within the church as a whole. If sin is "in the camp," we must find where it is hidden and then forcibly remove it.

In the Old Testament story in Joshua 7, Achan sinned by secretly coveting, stealing, and hiding some of the sacred things after the battle of Jericho that the Lord had commanded them not to take into their camp but to place them in His treasury. God warned them that His anger would fall upon them if they disobeyed His command. But Achan disobeyed and stole some of these things and hid them in the camp without anyone knowing about it, and the anger of the Lord indeed fell upon the Children of Israel. The Lord revealed Achan's sin to Joshua, who exposed the sin; and the Lord dealt with it in a seriously dramatic way. I encourage you to read the full story in your Bible. This story teaches us just how serious our hidden sin is in the eyes of our Holy God. The severity of God's action is also confirmed to believers in the New Testament:

> But because of your stubbornness and your unrepentant heart, you are storing up wrath against yourself for the day of God's wrath, when his righteous judgment will be revealed.
> —ROMANS 2:5, NIV

What God desires is to hear us admit and confess our hidden sins, to ask Him to cleanse us and forgive us of these things through the blood of Christ, and then to believe that He will do it. The purpose of confession and repentance of sin is not to make us feel guilty and condemned. It is actually God's way of making us holy.

Luke 11:10 says, "Everyone who asks, receives." We have an active part here. God tells us that in order to receive from Him we must ask of Him, not make gross assumptions that He will just give something to us when we can't even be bothered to open our mouths and ask Him. Such an attitude surely is taking the grace of God for granted.

Let me just say that living life as a true believer is not about constant perfection. It is all about having the right heart towards God—a heart that wants to obey God and yields to His will, valuing and cherishing His precious holy Word above all else. A true believer is a person who stands firm in the face of opposition and refuses to compromise the Word of God when pressured by the demands of this world to do so.

So let's now have a look at the wonderful things that the Word of God has promised to all those who are true believers. Oh, how these promises ought to keep us rooted in and obedient to God's holy Word! Receiving such glorious promises could be at stake if we treat biblical obedience as something which is outdated, irrelevant, and belonging to a bygone era. What the Lord promises to those who are true believers is breathtaking and beyond our ability to comprehend. But we need to grasp hold of the fact that His promises *are* real and *will* be fulfilled for those who truly love Him, follow Him, and worship Him in obedience to the very end.

> [Speaking to His twelve disciples] Jesus replied, "I assure you that when the world is made new and the Son of Man sits upon his glorious throne, you who have been my followers will also sit on twelve thrones, judging the twelve tribes of Israel. And everyone who has given up houses or brothers or sisters or father or mother or children or property, for my sake, will receive a hundred times as much in return and will inherit eternal life."
>
> —MATTHEW 19:28–29

> And then at last, the sign that the Son of Man is coming will appear in the heavens, and there will be deep mourning among all the peoples of the earth. And they will see the Son of Man coming on the clouds of heaven with power and great glory. And he will send out his angels with the mighty blast of a trumpet, and they will gather his chosen ones from

all over the world —from the farthest ends of the earth and heaven.

—Matthew 24:30-31

His master replied, "Well done, good and faithful servant! You have been faithful with a few things; I will put you in charge of many things. Come and share your master's happiness!"

—Matthew 25:23, niv

Then the King will say to those on his right, "Come, you who are blessed by my Father; take your inheritance, the kingdom prepared for you since the creation of the world."

—Matthew 25:34, niv

All those the Father gives me will come to me, and whoever comes to me I will never drive away. For I have come down from heaven not to do my will but to do the will of him who sent me. And this is the will of him who sent me, that I shall lose none of all those he has given me, but raise them up at the last day. For my Father's will is that everyone who looks to the Son and believes in him shall have eternal life, and I will raise them up at the last day.

—John 6:37-40, niv

Jesus said to her, "I am the resurrection and the life. The one who believes in me will live, even though they die; and whoever lives by believing in me will never die. Do you believe this?"

—John 11:25-26, niv

Do not let your hearts be troubled. You believe in God; believe also in me. My Father's house has many rooms; if that were not so, would I have told you that I am going there to prepare a place for you? And if I go and prepare a place for you, I will come back and take you to be with me that you also may be where I am.

—JOHN 14:1–3, NIV

But now that you have been set free from sin and have become slaves of God, the benefit you reap leads to holiness, and the result is eternal life. For the wages of sin is death, but the gift of God is eternal life in Christ Jesus our Lord.

—ROMANS 6:22–23, NIV

For if you live according to the flesh, you will die; but if by the Spirit you put to death the misdeeds of the body, you will live. For those who are led by the Spirit of God are the children of God…Now if we are children, then we are heirs—heirs of God and co-heirs with Christ, if indeed we share in his sufferings in order that we may also share in his glory. I consider that our present sufferings are not worth comparing with the glory that will be revealed in us.

—ROMANS 8:13–14, 17–18, NIV

And do this, understanding the present time: The hour has already come for you to wake up from your slumber, because our salvation is nearer now than when we first believed.

—ROMANS 13:11, NIV

No eye has seen, no ear has heard, and no mind has imagined what God has prepared for those who love him.

—1 CORINTHIANS 2:9

But someone will ask, "How are the dead raised? With what kind of body will they come?" How foolish! What you sow does not come to life unless it dies. When you sow, you do not plant the body that will be, but just a seed, perhaps of wheat or of something else. But God gives it a body as he has determined, and to each kind of seed he gives its own body. Not all flesh is the same: People have one kind of flesh, animals have another, birds another and fish another. There are also heavenly bodies and there are earthly bodies; but the splendor of the heavenly bodies is one kind, and the splendor of the earthly bodies is another.

The sun has one kind of splendor, the moon another and the stars another; and star differs from star in splendor. So will it be with the resurrection of the dead. The body that is sown is perishable, it is raised imperishable; it is sown in dishonor, it is raised in glory; it is sown in weakness, it is raised in power; it is sown a natural body, it is raised a spiritual body. If there is a natural body, there is also a spiritual body. So it is written: "The first man Adam became a living being"; the last Adam, a life-giving spirit. The spiritual did not come first, but the natural, and after that the spiritual. The first man was of the dust of the earth; the second man is of heaven. As was the earthly man, so are those who are of the earth; and as is the heavenly man, so also are those who are of heaven. And just as we have borne the image of the earthly man, so shall we bear the image of the heavenly man. I declare to you, brothers and sisters, that flesh and blood cannot inherit the kingdom of God, nor does the perishable inherit the imperishable. Listen, I tell you a mystery: We will not all sleep, but we will all be changed—in a flash, in the twinkling of an eye, at the last trumpet. For the trumpet will sound, the dead will be raised imperishable, and we will be changed. For the perishable must clothe itself with the imperishable, and the mortal with immortality.

—1 CORINTHIANS 15:35–53, NIV

Therefore we do not lose heart. Though outwardly we are wasting away, yet inwardly we are being renewed day by day. For our light and momentary troubles are achieving for us an eternal glory that far outweighs them all. So we fix our eyes not on what is seen, but on what is unseen, since what is seen is temporary, but what is unseen is eternal.

—2 CORINTHIANS 4:16–18, NIV

For we know that if the earthly tent we live in is destroyed, we have a building from God, an eternal house in heaven, not built by human hands. Meanwhile we groan, longing to be clothed instead with our heavenly dwelling, because when we are clothed, we will not be found naked. For while we are in this tent, we groan and are burdened, because we do not wish to be unclothed but to be clothed instead with our heavenly dwelling, so that what is mortal may be swallowed up by life. Now the one who has fashioned us for this very purpose is God, who has given us the Spirit as a deposit, guaranteeing what is to come. Therefore we are always confident and know that as long as we are at home in the body we are away from the Lord. For we live by faith, not by sight. We are confident, I say, and would prefer to be away from the body and at home with the Lord. So we make it our goal to please him, whether we are at home in the body or away from it. For we must all appear before the judgment seat of Christ, so that each of us may receive what is due us for the things done while in the body, whether good or bad.

—2 CORINTHIANS 5:1–10, NIV

But whatever were gains to me I now consider loss for the sake of Christ. What is more, I consider everything a loss because of the surpassing worth of knowing Christ Jesus my Lord, for whose sake I have lost all things. I consider them garbage, that I may gain Christ and be found in him, not having a righteousness of my own that comes from the law, but that which is through faith in Christ—the righteousness that comes from God on the basis of faith. I want to know Christ—yes, to know the power of his resurrection and participation in his sufferings, becoming like him in his death, and so, somehow, attaining to the resurrection from the dead. Not that I have already obtained all this, or have already arrived at my goal, but I press on to take hold of that for which Christ Jesus took hold of me. Brothers and sisters, I do not consider myself yet to have taken hold of it. But one thing I do: Forgetting what is behind and straining toward what is ahead, I press on toward the goal to win the prize for which God has called me heavenward in Christ Jesus.

—PHILIPPIANS 3:7–14, NIV

For, as I have often told you before and now tell you again even with tears, many live as enemies of the cross of Christ. Their destiny is destruction, their god is their stomach, and their glory is in their shame. Their mind is set on earthly things. But our citizenship is in heaven. And we eagerly await a Savior from there, the Lord Jesus Christ who, by the power that enables him to bring everything under his control, will transform our lowly bodies so that they will be like his glorious body.

—PHILIPPIANS 3:18–21, NIV

Once you were alienated from God and were enemies in your minds because of your evil behavior. But now he has reconciled you by Christ's physical body through death to present you holy in his sight, without blemish and free from accusation—*if you continue in your faith, established and firm, and do not move from the hope held out in the gospel.*

—COLOSSIANS 1:21–23A, NIV, EMPHASIS ADDED

Since, then, you have been raised with Christ, set your hearts on things above, where Christ is, seated at the right hand of God. Set your minds on things above, not on earthly things. For you died, and your life is now hidden with Christ in God. When Christ, who is your life, appears, then you also will appear with him in glory.

—COLOSSIANS 3:1–4, NIV

And now, dear brothers and sisters, we want you to know what will happen to the believers who have died so you will not grieve like people who have no hope. For since we believe that Jesus died and was raised to life again, we also believe that when Jesus returns, God will bring back with him the believers who have died. We tell you this directly from the Lord: We who are still living when the Lord returns will not meet him ahead of those who have died. For the Lord himself will come down from heaven with a commanding shout, with the voice of the archangel, and with the trumpet call of God. First, the Christians who have died will rise from their graves. Then, together with them, we who are still alive and remain on the earth will be caught up in the clouds to meet the Lord in the air. Then we will be with the Lord forever. So encourage each other with these words.

—1 Thessalonians 4:13–18

Now, brothers and sisters, about times and dates we do not need to write to you, for you know very well that the day of the Lord will come like a thief in the night…But you, brothers and sisters, are not in darkness so that this day should surprise you like a thief. You are all children of the light and children of the day. We do not belong to the night or to the darkness. So then, let us not be like others, who are asleep, but let us be awake and sober.

—1 Thessalonians 5:1–2, 4–6, niv

God is just: He will pay back trouble to those who trouble you and give relief to you who are troubled, and to us as well. This will happen when the Lord Jesus is revealed from heaven in blazing fire with his powerful angels.

—2 Thessalonians 1:6–7, niv

I have fought the good fight, I have finished the race, I have kept the faith. Now there is in store for me the crown of righteousness, which the Lord, the righteous Judge, will award to me on that day—and not only to me, but also to all who have longed for his appearing.

—2 Timothy 4:7–8, niv

For the grace of God has appeared that offers salvation to all people. It teaches us to say "No" to ungodliness and worldly passions, and to live self-controlled, upright and godly lives in this present age, while we wait for the blessed hope—the appearing of the glory of our great God and Savior, Jesus Christ, who gave himself for us to redeem us from all wickedness and to purify for himself a people that are his very own, eager to do what is good.

—Titus 2:11–14, NIV

But when the kindness and love of God our Savior appeared, he saved us, not because of righteous things we had done, but because of his mercy. He saved us through the washing of rebirth and renewal by the Holy Spirit, whom he poured out on us generously through Jesus Christ our Savior, so that, having been justified by his grace, we might become heirs having the hope of eternal life.

—Titus 3:4–7, NIV

But he has appeared once for all at the culmination of the ages to do away with sin by the sacrifice of himself. Just as people are destined to die once, and after that to face judgment, so Christ was sacrificed once to take away the sins of many; *and he will appear a second time, not to bear sin, but to bring salvation to those who are waiting for him.*

—Hebrews 9:26b–28, NIV, EMPHASIS ADDED

Blessed is the one who perseveres under trial because, having stood the test, that person will receive the crown of life that the Lord has promised to those who love him.

—James 1:12, NIV

Praise be to the God and Father of our Lord Jesus Christ! In his great mercy he has given us new birth into a living hope through the resurrection of Jesus Christ from the dead, and into an inheritance that can never perish, spoil or fade. This inheritance is kept in heaven for you, who through faith are shielded by God's power until the coming of the salvation that is ready to be revealed in the last time. In all this you greatly rejoice, though now for a little while you may have had to suffer grief in all kinds of trials. These have come so that the proven genuineness of your faith—of greater worth than gold, which perishes even though refined by fire—may result in praise, glory and honor when Jesus Christ is revealed. Though you have not seen him, you love him; and even though you do not see him now, you believe in him and are filled with an inexpressible and glorious joy, for you are receiving the end result of your faith, the salvation of your souls.

—1 Peter 1:3–9, niv

Therefore, my brothers and sisters, make every effort to confirm your calling and election. For if you do these things, you will never stumble, and you will receive a rich welcome into the eternal kingdom of our Lord and Savior Jesus Christ.

—2 Peter 1:10–11, niv

But the day of the Lord will come as unexpectedly as a thief. Then the heavens will pass away with a terrible noise, and the very elements themselves will disappear in fire, and the earth and everything on it will be found to deserve judgment. Since everything around us is going to be destroyed like this, what holy and godly lives you should live.

—2 Peter 3:10–11

Dear friends, now we are children of God, and what we will be has not yet been made known. But we know that when Christ appears, we shall be like him, for we shall see him as he is. All who have this hope in him purify themselves, just as he is pure.

—1 John 3:2–3, niv

Watch out that you do not lose what we have worked for, but that you may be rewarded fully.

—2 John 1:8, niv

Whoever has ears, let them hear what the Spirit says to the churches. To the one who is victorious, I will give the right to eat from the tree of life, which is in the paradise of God.

—REVELATION 2:7, NIV

Do not be afraid of what you are about to suffer. I tell you, the devil will put some of you in prison to test you, and you will suffer persecution for ten days. Be faithful, even to the point of death, and I will give you life as your victor's crown. Whoever has ears, let them hear what the Spirit says to the churches. The one who is victorious will not be hurt at all by the second death.

—REVELATION 2:10–11, NIV

Whoever has ears, let them hear what the Spirit says to the churches. To the one who is victorious, I will give some of the hidden manna. I will also give that person a white stone with a new name written on it, known only to the one who receives it.

—REVELATION 2:17, NIV

To the one who is victorious and does my will to the end, I will give authority over the nations—that one "will rule them with an iron scepter and will dash them to pieces like pottery"—just as I have received authority from my Father. I will also give that one the morning star.

—REVELATION 2:26–28, NIV

All who are victorious will be clothed in white. I will never erase their names from the Book of Life, but I will announce before my Father and his angels that they are mine.

—REVELATION 3:5

All who are victorious will become pillars in the Temple of my God, and they will never have to leave it. And I will write on them the name of my God, and they will be citizens in the city of my God—the new Jerusalem that comes down

from heaven from my God. And I will also write on them
my new name.

—REVELATION 3:12

Those who are victorious will sit with me on my throne, just
as I was victorious and sat with my Father on his throne.

—REVELATION 3:21

Look, I am coming soon! My reward is with me, and I will
give to each person according to what they have done. I
am the Alpha and the Omega, the First and the Last, the
Beginning and the End. Blessed are those who wash their
robes, that they may have the right to the tree of life and may
go through the gates into the city.

—REVELATION 22:12–14, NIV

There are many other promises awaiting true believers written
throughout the rest of the Book of Revelation, but I will not include
them again here in view of our study of the end of the world from
the Book of Revelation in chapter 3.

So, after reading all these things, all I can exclaim is, "Wow!
How wonderful! How amazing! How awesome!" Just reading them
all is so exciting. But just imagine how much more exciting it will
be when we arrive at the gates of heaven and hear those words,
"Well done, my good and faithful servant," and, "Come, you who
are blessed by My Father; take your inheritance, the kingdom prepared for you since the creation of the world" (Matt. 25:23, 34,
NIV). We will then be escorted into the city of gold and taken to
our heavenly mansion. Our joy will be beyond description.

Ryle writes,

Reader, who can tell the full nature of the inheritance of the
saint in light? Who can describe the glory which is yet to be
revealed and given to the children of God? Words fail us.
Language falls short. Mind cannot conceive fully, and tongue
cannot express perfectly, the things which are comprised in

the glory yet to come upon the sons and daughters of the Lord Almighty.[2]

However, many followers of Christ seem baffled by it all and can't get their heads around the glorious inheritance that awaits true believers. So, they put it out of their minds altogether or, worse still, they dismiss it as a fairy tale.

When we were little children we loved to hear stories like this. We were told they were only make-believe and were not reality; however, we still entered into the joyous experience of them, secretly dreaming and wishing that they could be a reality.

But the wonderful news is that all that the Word of God says about the awesome experience which awaits true believers in the kingdom of heaven is *not* a fairy tale. It is very real, and one day we will experience it for eternity.

Recall to mind the most wonderful fairy story you have ever heard and then magnify the beauty and joy of it about a million times. I am sure that will be only a fraction of what it will be like living forever in the presence of God in the kingdom of heaven.

Knowing what awaits us should excite us so much that we will want to obey God's Word in every area of our life. As we have seen in the scriptures, the inheritance and the promises that are laid up in the kingdom of heaven are for true believers who obey God's Word and overcome right up to the end. So, at this point, the joy I feel about it all must now once again turn to a warning. I would be failing in the work the Lord has given me to do if I neglected to continue with the warnings He has given and will continue to give right up until the end of the world.

As believers, we cannot afford to live our lives on earth with a halfhearted, lukewarm attitude towards our faith, towards our daily life in Christ, and to the urgent message to be watching and waiting for the signs of the approaching return of Christ and the final end of the world. Concerning followers of Christ living in this world while we wait for Jesus to return, Ryle writes,

I want to disqualify no man for usefulness upon the earth. I require no man to become a hermit, and cease to serve his generation. I call no man to leave his lawful calling and neglect his earthly affairs. But I do call everyone to live like one who expects Christ to return: to live soberly, righteously and godly in this present world; to live like a pilgrim and a stranger, ever looking unto Jesus; to live like a good servant, with his loins girded up, and his lamp burning; to live like one whose treasure is in heaven and his heart packed up and ready to be gone. This is readiness. This is preparation. And is this too much to ask? I say un-hesitantly that it is not. Now reader, are you ready in this way?[3]

If we live our lives with our minds focused on the prize that awaits us in heaven, we will find that we actually want to live lives that are pleasing to God in obedience to what His Word says. When we read all the incredible things that God wants to bestow upon those who are true believers, what believer would not want to receive them? How could we even permit any thoughts to take root in our minds and hearts of abandoning our faith, turning our backs on Jesus Christ, and forfeiting our right to enter into the kingdom of heaven?

To do so is to deliberately choose the opposite, which is eternal torment in hell. There are no streets of gold there. No rejoicing or singing in worship. No love, no light, no peace, no joy—only eternal pain, torment, weeping and wailing, tormenting heat and burning, fire, smoke, and thick darkness. It is a place where Satan and his demons will torment and mock all who end up there for refusing to believe in Jesus Christ when they had the opportunity to, *and* those who once believed but then abandoned their faith and entered fully back into the sins of the world and continued to live their lives according to the customs and practices of the unbelieving world, refusing to repent.

He will come with his mighty angels, in flaming fire, bringing judgment on those who don't know God *and on those who refuse to obey the Good News of our Lord Jesus.* They will be punished with eternal destruction, forever separated from the Lord and from his glorious power.

—2 Thessalonians 1:7b–9, emphasis added

Satan and his demons know that Jesus Christ is the Messiah, the King of kings and Lord of lords. They know that Jesus is the Son of God. They know that their eternal destiny is in the lake of fire; therefore, their evil desire is to take as many people as possible with them including rebellious, disobedient, and unrepentant believers—believers who have listened to and been deceived into believing the false doctrines of man that have been dressed up to look and sound like the truth.

Come on, church! Wake up!

Come on, believers! Wake up!

If you are a believer caught in unrepentant sin, *wake up now*! Drag yourself out of the mess you have fallen into. Fall on your face before God and confess your sin and repent of it all. Make a commitment to the Lord to obey His Word from this day forward. (See appendix B: "Prayer for Believers Caught in Unrepentant Sin.") Renounce whatever it is that you have entered into or attached yourself to or made an evil agreement with. Cut it off from your life.

If your hand causes you to sin, cut it off. It's better to enter eternal life with only one hand than to go into the unquenchable fires of hell with two hands. If your foot causes you to sin, cut it off. It's better to enter eternal life with only one foot than to be thrown into hell with two feet. And if your eye causes you to sin, gouge it out. It's better to enter the Kingdom of God with only one eye than to have two eyes and be thrown into hell, "where the maggots never die and the fire never goes out."

—MARK 9:43–48

In this passage Jesus is telling us in plain and simple language that if we are believers who refuse to cut off the things in our life that are sinful, our whole body will be cast into hell. If what we are doing with our hands is sinful, we must take action to stop doing those things. If our feet are taking us to places where no professing Christian should be seen, we must take radical action to stop ourselves from walking to those places. If our eyes are looking at things that we would be ashamed about if people discovered what we were seeing, we need to take drastic action to stop looking at these things. This is what Jesus means when He tells us to cut off our hand, cut off our foot, or gouge out our eye.

He was teaching His followers about how to live godly lives in order to enter the kingdom of heaven. There is no ambiguity about His words. They are as clear as the light of day, and His words categorically refute the deceiving "once saved, always saved" doctrine that is being preached in many churches today.

I often wonder how church leaders and individual believers are able to block these serious warnings out of their minds, and then just carry on doing whatever it is that causes them to sin. It would seem we are able to do this when we love being "engaged to sin" more than we love being "engaged to the One" to whom we are betrothed. Jesus is our Bridegroom. As believers, we are His bride. We are currently in the betrothal period, the period of our engagement to Him. We will become His true bride when He returns to redeem us and take us to our heavenly home to live with Him forever. But while we are in this engagement period, we must cut off our engagement to the things of this world that cause us to keep on sinning.

Make today a new day of renewing your vow of commitment to your Bridegroom, Jesus Christ. The Lord sees all that you have done and are still doing, and His heart grieves over your waywardness. He yearns for you to return to Him in confession and repentance. He holds out His arms of love and forgiveness towards you, but *you* are the one who must turn away from your sin. It is *you* who must turn around, walk back to your heavenly Father, and confess that you have sinned and you will now repent of it and turn back to living your life in accordance with His holy Word. As you do so, He will forgive you and cleanse you from all unrighteousness (1 John 1:9, KJV).

Why do we continue to choose to dice with death on a daily basis instead of obeying our loving Father who knows exactly what is best for us? We are talking about eternity in hell with relentless torment beyond imagination or description. Why would we continue to live lives that will reap such devastating eternal consequences when the Lord has already spread out His banqueting table for us to feast at when the great day of the marriage of the Lamb with His bride arrives?

The body of believers is His bride. But the bride must be ready for her wedding. She gets herself ready by confessing her daily sins, renouncing all involvement with the ways of the world, forsaking those ways, and repenting of them with determination and commitment. As the bride does this on a daily basis, the Lord forgives her and cleanses her from all her unrighteousness, continually making her wedding garment spotless and white. Our wedding garment is the robe of righteousness we were clothed with when we became born again by the Spirit of God.

Living in this predominantly secular and unbelieving world, how do we keep our wedding garment clean when we are faced with a constant barrage of evil that screams at us to partake of its "delicious fruits"? Jesus said to Peter, "A person who has bathed all over does not need to wash, except for the feet, to be entirely clean. And you disciples are clean" (John 13:10). (See the story in John 13:4–10.)

The apostle John said, "If we confess our sins, he is faithful and just to forgive us our sins, and to cleanse us from all unrighteousness" (1 John 1:9, KJV). Therefore, once we are born again and baptized and are clothed in our wedding garment, all we need to do when we get covered in the defilement of living in this world is "wash the dirt off our feet." This washing of our feet is the daily act of confessing and repenting of our daily sins. As we do this humbly before the Lord, He is faithful and just to forgive us of our sins and will cleanse us from all our unrighteousness. We really need to grasp the liberating truth of this wonderful, merciful, gracious gift of the Lord.

The reality is that every day we dirty and defile our wedding garment through our thoughtless, careless, and even deliberate actions, thoughts, and words. The Lord has instructed us what to do about it, but He can only fulfill His part in forgiving us and cleansing our wedding garment when we obediently do our part in coming before Him in confession and repentance. There is a divine order for us to follow, but we frequently want to find a shortcut. Taking shortcuts will not produce the required results.

Let's take the situation of the parent-child relationship. The heart of a loving parent aches with forgiveness and restoration towards their wayward, rebellious, and disobedient child. These things are embedded in the parent's soul, wanting to be displayed. But first there has to be action on the part of the erring child. The parent longs to hear the child acknowledge that they have done wrong, say that they are sorry, and ask for forgiveness. As they do so, the deeply embedded feelings of the parent rush to the surface and pour out like a flood towards their child. Forgiveness and restoration enfold their child like a warm, embracing blanket, making them feel loved, cherished, and secure. As the child feels and witnesses this forgiveness and restoration, they are then able to understand the need in relationships to be truthful about the mistakes they have made and to apologize for them to those who have been affected by the things they have said or done. The forgiveness and restoration given by the ones that have been hurt will help the child to make a commitment that they will not treat them this way again. A genuine apology always makes an offer of restitution towards those who have been affected by our actions. Making restitution says, "What can I do to repair the damage I have done?"

This parent-child scenario is how our relationship towards God ought to be. Many believers display the attitude of, "Oh, it doesn't matter if I keep messing up. God understands. He doesn't expect me to keep saying sorry for it. He has covered it all on the cross." This is an appalling attitude to have towards the Lord. It seems that many churches appear to be displaying this mindset, and it shocks me deeply. I am staggered that they have strayed so far from the Word of God on how to conduct relationships within the church and towards God.

Each of us should desire in our hearts to do the right thing towards our fellow brothers and sisters in Christ, and even towards our "enemies." Doing the right thing is doing what God's Word instructs us to do in the divine order that His Word has set. It is when we rebel and don't do the right thing towards others in the way that God has set that conflict and difficulties occur in relationships.

God expects us to deal with sin in our life and in our churches. Not dealing with sin is to condone it and allow it to take root. We have, in effect, given sin permission to dwell in our midst. When we give something permission, we are accepting its right to be there and to do what it wants. The more we permit sin to dwell and remain in our life or our church, the more entrenched it will become and the more destruction it will cause in our lives (see Galatians 6:8a).

Sin loves to dwell in the dark, unchecked. Sin does not want to be exposed. But when we come before God in brokenness, confession, and repentance for the sins we have allowed to remain in our lives, as an individual or as a whole church, this very action exposes sin before the throne of God. Sin's grip cannot remain once it has been exposed to the light of Christ. Confession and repentance brings the filthiness of our sins into Christ's powerful light. We are brought into a position where we are no longer able to hide ourselves. This is a *good* place to be. From this place of confession and repentance, God is able to set us free from the grip that our sins have had on us when we "fed" our sins in darkness. Praise God! However, if we *continue* to meddle in sin, as a believer, it will ultimately have devastating consequences for us spiritually and eternally. We have got to wake up to this truth.

When Jesus returns, we do not want to be found still wallowing in the sinful ways of the world—a world that refuses to believe in Him and has rejected anything to do with Him. As I have shown from scripture many times already, believers who are not ready when Jesus returns will not enter the kingdom of heaven. Jesus will shut the door on them (see Matthew 25:10–13).

This chapter was intended to share the joys of eternity in heaven awaiting all those who are true believers. Are you a true believer? Does your life inwardly and outwardly demonstrate the evidence of what the Lord requires of those who profess to be followers of Christ? If not, are you going to do something about it, or are you still going to believe a "gospel of deception" that pampers what your ears want to hear; a gospel that feeds you the lie that you don't need to bother confessing and repenting of the sins that still dwell in your life? In these end times, the church appears to be craving after a message that makes them feel comfortable. They are fulfilling the scripture that says,

> Now the Holy Spirit tells us clearly that in the last times some will turn away from the true faith; they will follow deceptive spirits and teachings that come from demons.
> —1 Timothy 4:1

But such teachings are leading the flock through the wide gate and onto the broad road that leads to destruction (Matt. 7:13, NIV).

Only obedience to the powerful, true, and often extremely uncomfortable message of the Word of God will lead us through the narrow gate and onto the straight path that leads to eternal life.

> You can enter God's kingdom only through the narrow gate. The highway to hell is broad, and its gate is wide for the many who choose that way. But the gateway to life is very narrow and the road is difficult, and only a few ever find it.
> —MATTHEW 7:13–14

These are not my words. They are Jesus' words. He says, "Few there be that find it" (v. 14, KJV). Put these verses next to all the ones where Jesus says that many who call Him, "Lord, Lord," will not enter the kingdom of heaven; this ought to cause everyone who professes to be a follower of Christ to examine their lives before God and take whatever steps are necessary to make themselves ready for Jesus' return.

Pastor Seung Woo Byun, in his book *Christians Going to Hell*, says (starting with the passage from Matthew 7:21–23):

> "Not everyone who says to me, 'Lord, Lord,' will enter the Kingdom of Heaven, but only he who does the will of my Father who is in heaven. Many will say to me on that day, 'Lord, Lord, did we not prophecy in your name, and in your name drive out demons and perform many miracles?' Then I will tell them plainly, 'I never knew you. Away from me you evildoers!'"
>
> Therefore, what Jesus is saying through this analogy is clear. No matter how much we confess our faith (v. 21), no matter how much we act like prophets, cast out demons, and perform miracles (vv. 22–23), no matter how much we listen to God's Word and understand it, even if we heard it through Jesus Himself, we will be judged, destroyed, and thrown into hell if we do not live by the Word. No one can change these words. These are the Lord's own words.[4]

Byun uses strong words indeed! So, it is very clear that, when Jesus returns, only those who are ready for His appearing (true believers) will be raised up to meet Him in the air. The rest of the believers who have *not* made themselves ready will be left behind. Based on Jesus' words in Matthew 24:40–41, this could be 50 percent. He says one will be taken and the other left.

Taking this literally, it could mean that in every church, half the congregation will be raised up to meet the Lord in the air and the other half will be left behind to face the Tribulation that will come upon the earth after the Rapture. Let's put it like this: if a church is preaching the Word of God without compromise and the entire congregation of that church is living their lives in readiness for Jesus' return, that entire congregation will be raised up on the day He returns. But, if another church is preaching a compromised version of the gospel, never warning the believers that hell is real and that they need to be watching for the signs of Jesus' return nor exhorting them to make sure they are living obedient and holy lives, then it is highly possible that they will all be left behind to face the Tribulation.

This very real possibility should shock us all because this could literally be the case. Church leaders and members may pretend their sins don't exist or try to hide them, but Jesus can see everything that is going on. "The Lord's light penetrates the human spirit, exposing every hidden motive" (Prov. 20:27). He is warning us all in the strongest possible terms what our outcome will be if we do not repent and get ourselves right with Him before He returns.

As a global body of believers, we should be falling on our faces in shame and repentance. Do we *really* love our Bridegroom? Do we *really* want to be His bride and be raised up to meet Him in the air on the day of His return? Do we *really* want to enter into the marriage feast with Him and live with Him forever?

I feel sure that our heavenly Father is delaying His Son's return because He sees His bride is not really ready to be united with her

Bridegroom. He sees her still mucking around in the "pigsty" of the world that does not want to know about God. He sees that her wedding garment is covered with the filth of her involvement with the sins of the world. He loves His bride but is warning her that He cannot allow her to enter into the marriage feast with Him if she continues to spurn His loving correction and fails to get herself ready for His return. The Bridegroom has spent eternity preparing a place for her in His heavenly kingdom, but it seems His bride is more interested in having a "last fling" with the world before her wedding day, more interested in carrying on with her "hen party" until the very last minute.

If she continues to do this, she may find herself in a drowsy, drunken slumber when the shout is raised, "Behold, the bridegroom cometh!" (Matt. 25:6, KJV.) She will not be able to lift up her head in rejoicing that her "redemption draweth nigh" (Luke 21:28, KJV). Her wedding garment is defiled because of her unconfessed and unrepentant sins. She will not be ready to meet the One who truly loves her, who gave His life for her. She will watch as the faithful and ready ones are welcomed into the wedding feast while she is left outside the door and not permitted entry. Her eternal state will be unchangeable—she will never be married to her Bridegroom. Her eternal destiny will be where she never expected to find herself, and she will weep and wail and gnash her teeth in distress and torment that she failed to heed the warnings to repent, keep watch, and get herself ready.

This may be the state for much of the church if it fails to take the Word of God seriously, failing to handle it and obey it with reverential fear and trembling. If we are "slumbering" believers wallowing around in the things of this world, we cannot expect to receive our Father's inheritance until we return to Him, like the Prodigal Son (see Luke 15:11–32).

It was only in returning to his father, confessing that he had sinned against him, and humbling himself before him that his father was able to forgive and restore his son. All the time that the son was wallowing around in the pigsty of life in the world he was not in the position to receive the forgiveness and the restoration that his father longed to give him. The son had to come to his senses and realize that what he was doing was sinful and that he needed to return to his father, hoping that he would at least give him the position of a hired hand. But his genuine godly sorrow and repentant actions caused his father to totally forgive him and restore him to his rightful place as his son.

This is what God will do for all believers when we fall into sin *but* then come to our senses and return to Him with a broken and contrite heart seeking His mercy, forgiveness, and restoration. But we absolutely *must* come to our senses about the sins we are committing and turn away from them and walk back to our Father. He waits for us to do this, and He watches for our return; but *we* must do the returning. Yes, the Prodigal Son's father still loved him while he was wallowing in the sinful lifestyle of the world. But the son could not be restored in his relationship with his father *until* he had come face-to-face with the reality of his sin and then made the conscious decision that he needed to return to his father with a heart of brokenness and repentance.

God still loves us when we have wandered off into "the wilderness of sin," but like the Prodigal Son, our relationship with our heavenly Father cannot be restored until we too come face-to-face with the reality of the sins we are continuing to commit as believers. And likewise, we need to make the conscious decision to return to God with a heart of brokenness and repentance.

Returning to the issue of "one will be taken, the other left" (Matt. 24:41), the same 50 percent applies in Jesus' parable about the ten virgins (see Matthew 25:1–13). We need to remember, all ten of them were followers of the Bridegroom and all of them knew that He would return at some point, but only five of them were keeping watch and had made sure they were ready for the His return. Only these five went into the marriage, and then the door was shut.

The other five followers of the Bridegroom, who had not kept watch and had not made themselves ready for whenever He returned, suddenly had a frantic panic when they heard the shout that the Bridegroom was coming. They found themselves outside the door and began to knock and asked the Bridegroom to open it, but the Bridegroom would not let them in and told them to go away as He did not know them. What a shock that ought to be to us! Both these scriptures (Matthew 24:40–42, 25:1–13) are referring to followers of the Bridegroom—that means those who profess to be Christians.

In relation to Jesus' parable about the ten virgins (see Matthew 25:1–13), Ryle says,

> It stands as a beacon to the Church of Christ in all ages. It is a witness against carelessness and slothfulness, against apathy and indifference, and a witness of no uncertain sound. It cries to the thoughtless, "Awake!" It cries to the true servants of Christ, "Watch!"[5]

Further, Ryle says this,

> I ask you, "Are you ready?" Remember the words of the Lord Jesus, 'They that were ready went in with the Bridegroom to the marriage': they that were ready and none else. Now here, in the sight of God, I ask each and every reader, is this your case? Are you ready?...I don't ask whether you are a churchman, and make a profession of religion. I do not ask whether you attend an evangelical ministry...and can talk on evangelical subjects...I want to search your heart more thoroughly, and probe your conscience more deeply. I want to know   whether you have been born again, and whether you have got the Holy Ghost dwelling in your soul. I want to know whether you have any oil in your vessel while you carry the lamp of profession, and whether you are ready to meet the Bridegroom, ready for Christ's return to earth. I

want to know, if the Lord should come this week, whether
you could lift up your head with joy and say, "This is our
God; we have waited for Him; let us be glad and rejoice in
His salvation." These things I want to know, and this is what
I mean when I say, "Are you ready?"[6]

Many churches today seem to be preaching a gospel that says
that everyone who professes to be a believer will be raised up on
the day of Jesus' return. This is *contrary* to what Jesus says.

In his book *Go and Sin No More*, Michael L. Brown speaks of
God's warning signs to believers that should bring about a conviction of sin when we are beginning to become desensitized to the
conviction of the Holy Spirit:

> The fact that something does not "bother you" may be the
> loudest warning you will ever get. Can you sin freely and not
> feel grief? Then fall on your face and cry for mercy before
> it's too late. Otherwise you might disqualify yourself from
> receiving the prize.[7]

How true this is. We may fall back into a sin that we used to
enjoy before we became a Christian. The first time we do so, the
Lord convicts us and we feel grief and shame about it. We say we
are sorry to the Lord; but if we fail to repent of it and thoroughly
turn away from it, we will open the door to Satan, who will come
in and take up residence in our life and tempt us to repeat that sin.

The more we repeat it, the more we desensitize our spirit to the
eternal consequences of repeated, unrepentant sin. God may try to
convict us a few more times; but if we fail to respond to His loving
grace of conviction, then there may come a point where we are
totally numb to any attempts by the Lord to convict us. If we are
able to sin freely without the slightest twinge of guilt, shame, or
grief at what we are doing, then we surely must be in a most dangerous place spiritually. The fact that we are able to not even wince
at the sins we are committing must surely cause us to realize that

we are on the road to spiritual suicide. The *absence* of *any* feelings of conviction within us has got to be the biggest red warning light that God could ever give us.

Jesus says that many shepherds will try to lead the sheep into the kingdom of heaven through a different gate, but that this will lead them to destruction. Jesus is the *only* gate into the kingdom of heaven (see John 10:1-15). But once we have become a believer by entering the gate through faith in Jesus Christ, we must then live our lives in obedience to *all* of His Word and not twist it and shape it to suit our preferences.

Scripture warns us not to turn to the right or to the left but to walk in all the ways that the Lord has commanded us (Deut. 5:32, KJV). Many will say that obedience is difficult. It is only difficult to obey when our flesh wants to do the opposite of obey. But when we do begin to obey, God transforms the initial difficulty into a delight to do His will (Ps. 40:8).

If you are a believer caught up in sin and are hiding it and making excuses for it, or even justifying it, God has a word for you: "Whoever conceals their sins does not prosper, but the one who confesses and renounces them will find mercy" (Prov. 28:13, NIV). Confession and repentance brings God's mercy, forgiveness, and restoration. To renounce something means that you have made a purposeful and deliberate decision of your will to cut off the things that you were involved in and to no longer associate yourself with them. To repent of something means that you are now making a purposeful and deliberate decision to turn away from those things and to turn back to Christ with a change of heart and mind to live your life in obedience to God's Word.

Confession and repentance are inseparable. They go hand in hand. If we merely confess our sins to God without repenting of them, it is very likely that we will keep on repeating our sinful behavior. This makes a mockery of the action of confessing our sins to God and asking Him to forgive us of what we have just done when we have no real intention or desire to turn away from those sins. When the temptation presents itself to us again, we will have no strength to overcome it because we have no desire to actually repent of it. To be brutally honest, when we adopt this sort of attitude before God, we are really behaving like selfish individuals. We want to come groveling to God, saying that we are sorry again, wanting Him to forgive us again, but actually don't want to give up the very things we keep on confessing to Him.

What sort of followers of Christ are we, if we just assume that God will continue to forgive us when we repeatedly confess the same sins to Him without any intention of renouncing and repenting of them? To ask someone to forgive you of the things you have done which have hurt and offended them and then to carry on doing those things over and over again is utter cruelty. In fact, I would go so far as to say it is downright evil. The fact that we do it to them again and again demonstrates to them that we really don't care what effect our behavior has on them. It says to them in unspoken words, "I am really sorry I have blown it again, but it is far easier for me to keep asking you to forgive me over and over again (even though it hurts you each time I do it) than it is for me to actually stop doing it. It's easier for you to forgive me than it is for me to do the hard work necessary to stop sinning against you. I don't really want to do that sort of hard work, so let me just carry on sinning and then saying sorry to you, even though I have no intention of doing anything about it."

This sort of attitude is a cop-out and is the total opposite of what God requires of us when we sin. We are to confess our sin, repent of it, and change our heart, our mind, and our behavior to that which is in keeping with the holy Word of God.

Byun writes,

> What is repentance? Many people think that repentance is cutting off sin. This is partly true, but not completely true. As Matthew 3:8 records, we must "produce fruit in keeping with repentance." The Greek word for repentance is *metanoia*, and

it means "change of heart" or "change of mind." Repentance is changing one's heart and mind. This is repentance, which naturally and inevitably leads to a change of behavior and speech—the fruit of repentance.[8]

The apostle Paul confirms this, "I preached that they should repent and turn to God and demonstrate their repentance by their deeds" (Acts 26:20b, NIV). So, clearly, without repentance there cannot be any possibility of a change in our thoughts, our words, or our deeds. There cannot be any possibility of a change in our hearts, our minds, or our behavior because such fruit is only borne through genuine repentance. Just saying the words, "I repent of my sins," is unlikely to have any lasting effect. True repentance comes from a place of godly sorrow for the sins we have committed (2 Cor. 7:10, NIV). This is a place of complete and utter brokenness before the Lord.

I was taken through this experience suddenly in October 2011. It was the most agonizing and overwhelming experience the Lord has ever taken me through in my twenty-one years as a Christian. My first book, *Come on Church! Wake Up!*, details this event fully.

So, where sin is concerned, we need to adopt a ruthless attitude towards its existence in our life. We must grab it by the scruff of the neck and kick it out of our life, not take it by the hand and "dance with the devil." This is exactly what we are doing when we give in to sin. As believers, each time we fall into sin we are saying to our Bridegroom that His love for us is not enough; we want something else to satisfy us as well. We let go of our Bridegroom's hand and take hold of the hand of the enemy, the one who is enticing us to partake of the evil deeds of darkness.

Our Bridegroom stands by and watches us, calling out to us, sending us warning signs that we are heading in the wrong direction, even shouting at us if necessary. But He will not force us to stop. That has to be our decision. We are the ones who have to respond to His instruction to stop, turn around, walk away from the sin, confess the sin, renounce it, and repent of it. Then we will produce the fruit that is in keeping with repentance (Matt. 3:8, NIV).

Brown says,

> Because we have died to our old life and now live a new life in Jesus, we must put to death…everything that pertains to the old, earthly life, putting on the new self. [Referring to Colossians 3:5–10, he then says]…Notice this is a command, not an option. It is a requirement for all believers, not a suggested goal for super saints.[9]

Further, he says,

> The life we are called to is beautiful, pure, clean, righteous and holy. The life we leave behind is ugly, impure, filthy, unrighteous and unholy. That's what God means when He calls us to stop sinning: Make a break with the old and walk in the new, offering our bodies as living sacrifices holy and pleasing to God, not conforming any longer to the pattern of this world, but being transformed by the renewing of our minds (see Romans 12:12). There is no acceptable middle ground.[10]

And again he says,

> It is absolutely essential that we recognize there is a complete contrast between the works of the flesh and the fruit of the Spirit. We should have nothing to do with the former and everything to do with the latter, our lives being characterized by Spirit-led, flesh-crucifying conduct and attitude.[11]

And again,

> So rather than make excuses for sin or looking for escape clauses to justify habitual compromise, we should be looking

for God's solutions to overcome sinful living and to His divine ways of escape from bondage to the flesh.[12]

And finally, Dr. Brown has some hopeful words for believers caught in sin:

> The Lord actually loves to love us. He delights in showing mercy (see Micah. 7:17–19; Ezekiel 18:23, 30–32; 33:11). He takes pleasure in forgiving. If you sin, the Lord wants you to come to Him in repentance. That's what He desires! He is not sick and tired of hearing your voice. He does not wish that you would just go away. "What if I keep blowing it?" you ask. I tell you again: He would rather hear your voice in sincere repentance—even if that repentance needs to go much deeper than it has so far—than not hear your voice at all. [13]

If you are a believer caught up in unrepentant sin, please *wake up*! Hear and obey the voice of the Bridegroom and respond to His merciful, forgiving and restoring love for you—before it is too late.

Chapter 7
THE END OF THE WORLD
FOR UNBELIEVERS

For I am not ashamed of the gospel of Christ: for it is the
power of God unto salvation to every one that believeth.

—ROMANS 1:16, KJV

THE FIRST THING I want to say to anyone who does not believe in God or His Son, Jesus Christ is that God loves you, even though you do not believe in Him or even believe that He exists. Whatever the reasons are for your unbelief, the truth is that God is real, He exists, He created the whole universe, and He created you (see Genesis 1–2; John 1:1–3). The following is the truth about our existence, how sin entered into the world, and God's gracious and merciful solution to the problem.

When God created the human race (see Genesis 1:26–27; 2:21–22), He created man and woman in His own image. At that time the human race started out in perfect harmony with God. There was no sin or evil within mankind at that point. When God looked at what He created, He saw that it was good (1:31). He loved what He created, and His desire and intention was to have a committed relationship with mankind. In order for this to happen, God had to set a boundary for them that He commanded them to obey. Their obedience would ensure the continuance of this perfect relationship between them and God.

God's boundary to the first human beings (Adam and Eve) was that they must not eat the fruit of the tree of the knowledge of good and evil; He warned them if they did, they would die (Gen.

2:16–17). God knew that if they ate that fruit they would suddenly gain knowledge of evil; and thus being exposed to its existence, they would be able to choose to do evil rather than obey God's will to do good. God told them that they could eat the fruit from any other tree in the Garden of Eden, but not the fruit from the tree of the knowledge of good and evil. It was a command that He wanted them to obey for their own eternal protection. He knew if they disobeyed His command, their disobedience would spoil their relationship with Him forever and would ultimately cause their spiritual death.

The devil, also known as Satan (who is not some fictitious character like so many books and films would have us believe), previously dwelt in heaven and was an archangel known as Lucifer. He became full of pride and desired to exalt himself above God. Because of his rebellion, the Lord cast him out of heaven and down to the earth. (See Isaiah 14:12–15, KJV.)

Satan disguised himself as a serpent and entered the Garden of Eden, and tempted Eve to eat the fruit of the tree of the knowledge of good and evil. He deceived her into believing that it would actually be good for her to eat it. Adam was standing by while his wife was being tempted and deceived by the devil, and he did nothing to prevent it. In fact, Eve handed the fruit to her husband to eat it too. The moment they disobeyed God's command by eating this "forbidden fruit," the disposition of sin entered into them. They were immediately convicted of their disobedience and hid themselves from God. Because of their rebellion against the loving boundary and command that God had set for them, He had to banish them from the Garden of Eden. The Garden was a place of paradise and perfection, and God could not allow anything sinful or evil to dwell in it. So Adam and Eve were banished from it forever and the Lord put angels at the gates with flaming swords, to bar them from ever entering it again. God told Adam that he must now spend the rest of his days toiling away in order to provide food to eat. He would have to work hard on the land to produce food by the sweat of his brow. (See Genesis 3.)

Adam and Eve had children (see Genesis 4). From the outset the consequence of their rebellion against God's first command can be seen throughout the generations that have existed from their first children Cain and Abel to the present day. It is clear that, once sin entered into the heart of the human race due to Adam's and Eve's disobedience to God's holy command, every single person born from that moment on has been born with the disposition of sin within them.

While a newborn baby looks perfect in every way, as it grows and develops into a toddler, the desire to have its own way becomes clearly evident by the age of two. The child is capable of throwing incredible tantrums in its frustration to get what it wants. When my daughter Emma was born, I could not get her to fall asleep without a pacifier in her mouth. I did not mind this at all, and I had three different ones so that there was always a clean one to hand if the one she was using dropped on the floor. But around the age of two, things started to get a bit complicated. Because the pacifiers were different colors, she decided she wanted to have two at bedtime so that she could see which one she liked best. She would not go to sleep until she had both of them.

After a few weeks she then wanted all three of them. I resisted for a few days and endured her constant cries of, "Mummy! Mummy! I want my dummy!" (*dummy* is the English word for a pacifier.) After I could stand it no longer, I gave her all three to see what would happen. I would peek through the gap in her door where I left it slightly open, and she would be playing a game with the pacifiers, popping one in her mouth, then another, and finally the last one, until all three of them were sticking out of her little mouth. On one occasion she noticed me peeking through the door and she grinned at me with her infectious, cheeky grin, and I could not help but laugh.

But somehow, at the age of two, I had to explain to her that her little game of control had to come to an end. I lovingly told her that it was time to wave bye-bye to her dummies. I did this slowly so as not to cause her to throw a huge tantrum. On the day the garbage men came, I helped her put one of them in the garbage can, and then we waved bye-bye to it as the garbage truck drove away. After shedding a few tears, she was fine. She knew she still had two left, and so she went to sleep with them without any trouble.

The same procedure occurred the following week, again with a few tears as we waved bye-bye to the second one. Now she was down to just one left. I was dreading the following week when the garbage men arrived. But she surprised me immensely. She eagerly put the last one in the garbage can, happily waved bye-bye to it, and then went off and played with some of her toys without shedding a single tear. When it was time for bed, she jumped under the covers, cuddled her favorite toys, and fell asleep without a single mention of the pacifiers.

While this situation seems cute and funny, many parents face behavior from their children that is much worse than the little personal story I have shared—behavior that seems to be beyond their control. Whether our young child's behavior is naughty but cute, or naughty, manipulative, and destructive, it is the early evidence of the inherent disposition of sin that all human beings are born with because of the disobedience of Adam and Eve (see Romans 5:12–19).

In the Old Testament, King Solomon recorded several proverbs concerning the outcome of a child's behavior when they are left to their own devices. These also instruct us that bringing up our children in the training and admonition of the Lord will correct their behavior.

> Foolishness is bound in the heart of a child; but the rod of correction shall drive it far from him.
>
> —PROVERBS 22:15, KJV

> A rod and a reprimand impart wisdom, but a child left undisciplined disgraces its mother.
>
> —PROVERBS 29:15, NIV

We are all born with this disposition of inherent sin. It is obvious that this is the case when we witness the escalating violence and destruction in families, society, and the world as a whole. God did not create mankind with the nature of sin. Sin entered the human race through mankind's first rebellion of God's loving command which He had set for our eternal protection.

The consequence of this falls upon all mankind, from the least to the greatest. We are born with the disposition to sin. But, as God says that nothing sinful or evil will ever be allowed to enter the kingdom of heaven, it would appear then that the entire human race is in a desperate spiritual dilemma. When we die, it would seem that we are doomed to living forever *outside* the kingdom of heaven, in a place where sin is eagerly accepted. In the Bible this place is called hell. It is the kingdom of Satan and his demons.

Because we are born with the disposition of sin, as hard as this is to comprehend, hell is actually our eternal destiny by default. So, therefore, if we do not want to find ourselves in this tormenting place where everything that is sinful and evil is accepted, it makes sense that the disposition of sin that we are all born with *must* be removed from our hearts. A transformation *must* take place within us. If we reject or resist this lifesaving transformation, then the inherent disposition of sin will remain in us and our end will be eternity in hell, since nothing sinful and evil will be allowed to enter the kingdom of heaven.

Our disposition of inherent sin cannot be eradicated by our own efforts. God has provided the answer, the antidote, which is the shed blood of Jesus Christ on the cross. The blood of Jesus Christ will cleanse you and wash away the filth of your sins. It will purify you, forgive you, heal you, and restore you.

He himself bore our sins in his body on the cross, so that we might die to sins and live for righteousness; "by his wounds you have been healed."

—1 PETER 2:24, NIV

It will make you into a new creation in Christ Jesus and will redeem you from the kingdom of darkness and transfer you into the kingdom of light, which is the kingdom of His dear Son, Jesus Christ (Col. 1:13). Halleluiah!

This has been done for the whole of mankind in every nation on earth, *but* we cannot just claim this as an automatic right. We can only receive this freedom and the inheritance of eternal life in the kingdom of heaven by confessing and repenting of our sins and believing and trusting in the One who died on the cross—the One who shed His precious blood to make this all possible. Who is that One? Jesus Christ is His name. He is the Son of God. He is the Messiah, the Savior of all who will believe and trust in Him, and obey the holy Word of God.

In the July 24th entry of his book *My Utmost for His Highest*, Oswald Chambers writes the following concerning this very matter:

> His Nature and Our Motives: "...unless your righteousness exceeds the righteousness of the scribes and Pharisees, you will by no means enter the kingdom of heaven" (Matthew 5:20).
>
> The characteristic of a disciple is not that he does good things, but that he is good in his motives, having been made good by the supernatural grace of God. The only thing that exceeds right *doing* is right *being*. Jesus Christ came to place within anyone who would let him a new heredity that would have a righteousness exceeding that of the scribes and Pharisees. Jesus is saying. "If you are My disciple, you must be right not only in your actions, but also in your motives, your aspirations, and in the deep recesses of the thoughts of your

mind." Your motives must be so pure that God Almighty can see nothing to rebuke. Who can stand in the eternal light of God and have nothing for Him to rebuke? Only the Son of God, and Jesus Christ claims that through His redemption He can place within anyone His own nature and make that person as pure and as simple as a child. The purity that God demands is impossible unless I can be remade within, and that is exactly what Jesus has undertaken to do through His redemption.

No one can make himself pure by obeying laws. Jesus Christ does not give us rules and regulations—He gives us His teachings which are truths that can only be interpreted by His nature which He places within us. The great wonder of Jesus Christ's salvation is that He changes our heredity. He does not change human nature—He changes its source, and thereby its motives as well.[1]

So, when we turn to God, believe the truth of the transaction that took place on the cross of Christ to set us free from our inherent disposition of sin, and put our faith in Jesus Christ to change our heredity, only then will we be set free from the "seed" of the disposition of sin that Satan planted into the entire human race when he deceived Adam and Eve in the garden of Eden.

Each of us on our own must come to this place before the throne of God. If we fail to do this, the inherent disposition of sin will remain in us. And when we die, we will die in sin (see Ezekiel 33:9; John 8:24) and our eternal destiny will be in hell; because, as we have seen, nothing sinful will be allowed into the kingdom of heaven. The apostle John confirms the inherent condemnation of all mankind who do not believe in the only begotten Son of God;

> Whoever believes in him is not condemned, but whoever does not believe stands condemned already because he has not believed in the name of God's one and only Son.
>
> —John 3:18, niv

So, if you are not a believer but are still of the belief that you will go to a "better place" when you die, I would like to encourage you to continue reading this chapter. God's Word has much to say about what will happen to those who remain unbelievers. He doesn't say it to condemn unbelievers; He says it out of His deepest heart of love for you, to warn you where your unbelief will lead you in the final outcome. God does not want anyone to perish. But none of us will go to that "better place" when we die if we continually resist and reject the truth that God is revealing to us about Jesus Christ.

Throughout the Bible God is warning us about the devastating reality of the eternal fires of hell. At the same time God is showing us where the "Fire Exit" is. Jesus Christ *is* the "Fire Exit." He is the door that stands permanently open, willing all humanity to accept, believe, and trust in what He has accomplished on the cross for our salvation. He longs for us to believe the truth that He is the only One who can save us from the eternal fires of hell that await all who will not believe and obey His Word. While the fire exit door of salvation through faith in Jesus Christ stands permanently open, Jesus will not force us to escape through it. The decision to escape the fires of hell is our decision alone.

Although, as an unbeliever your life might be relatively "good" without much outward evidence of sinful behavior or activity, it is easy to fall into the deception that you are okay and will go to that "better place" when you die. Without Christ you still have the inherent disposition of sin within you; and unless you turn to Christ to save you and set you free from sin, no matter how "morally upright" your life might appear right now, you will not go to heaven when you die.

Many people in this world appear morally upright but still reject Jesus Christ as the only way to be saved. Our moral uprightness can lead to pride. It deceives us into believing that we don't need God. We may say, "I am a good person. I don't murder, I don't steal, I don't lie, I give to charity, I help my neighbour. Of course God will let me into heaven when I die!"

Dear reader, God doesn't look at your earthly moral upright-ness to determine whether you will enter heaven when you die, although doing good is an important outworking for those who have put their faith and trust in Jesus for salvation (see Ephesians 2:10). God looks at your heart and sees the disposition of sin that is a part of you from the moment of your conception. He sees that you have not come before Him to ask Him to set you free from the disposition of sin by accepting Jesus Christ as your only means of salvation and deliverance.

God sees the resistance in your heart and your continual striving to "prove" to yourself and to Him that you are *not* a sinner. God's Word says that all have sinned and fallen short of the glory of God (Rom. 3:23). If God's Word says that we are all sinners in need of salvation through the only means He has made possible—through faith and trust in Jesus Christ, we ought to ask ourselves why we continually reject His Word and try to prove to God that His Word on this matter is wrong. We ought to examine why we stubbornly and proudly insist that we are okay and believe that we will get into heaven without the salvation that God has made available to us through Jesus Christ. Trying to prove to God that we are good enough to get into heaven will *not* get us into heaven. This fact is a biblical truth. It is unchangeable.

So in this chapter we will look at the Scriptural evidence that clearly shows the eternal destiny of all who do not believe, those who refuse to believe, and also those who once believed but have now turned their back on faith in Jesus Christ and are now living their lives in rebellion and disobedience to the Word of God.

The belief we are talking about is not just belief in anything we choose. It is belief that Jesus Christ is the Son of God. It is the belief that the purpose of His birth, death on the cross, burial, resurrection, and ascension into heaven was ordained by God to open up the way for all mankind to be reconciled to God eternally through confession and repentance of their sins. It is the belief that putting our faith in Jesus Christ will save us from the consequences of sin, which is eternity in hell.

"All mankind" means *everyone*. That means every man, every woman, and every child from every race, tribe, color, and creed from every nation, every city, every town, every village, every street, and every house. God does not want anyone to perish but desires that *all* would come to repentance (2 Pet. 3:9, NIV). It is therefore clear that if we do not repent, we will perish. Let this truth sink into the depths of our beings. If we do not want to perish, we need to repent of our sins, turn to God, and put our faith in Jesus Christ to save us. Jesus is the *only* name by which we can be saved (Acts 4:12).

If we die as an unbeliever, without Jesus Christ as our Lord and Savior, we will not enter the kingdom of heaven. The kingdom of heaven is the eternal dwelling place of God and His Son, Jesus Christ. So it would seem obvious that someone who does not believe in God and Jesus and who does not want to accept His Word as the truth would feel completely uncomfortable and out of place living in the kingdom of heaven for eternity.

It would be excruciating for an unbeliever to be in the glorious presence of the Lord in whom they refused to believe. They would not be able to cope with the unending praise and worship being poured out to God and His Son, Jesus Christ, from those who believe. The fact that someone is an unbeliever means that there is only one place where their unbelief will be accepted and eagerly received—that is the place called hell.

The Scriptures show that all unbelievers will end up in hell, regardless of whether they have lived their life as "good" unbelievers or "bad" unbelievers. In the eyes of the Lord, the deciding factor will be whether or not you are a true believer in Jesus Christ. If we are an unbeliever and are still alive on the earth when Jesus returns and the end of the world comes, the same deciding factor will apply. At that point if we do not believe that Jesus Christ is the Messiah, the Savior, and the Son of God and we have refused to put our trust in Him to save us from the eternal consequences that await all those who do not believe, we can hardly expect Him to make an exception for us when that terrible Day of Judgment comes.

The time to decide is now. This very minute!

> As God's partners, we beg you not to accept this marvelous gift of God's kindness and then ignore it. For God says, "At just the right time, I heard you. On the day of salvation, I helped you." Indeed, the "right time" is now. Today is the day of salvation.
>
> —2 Corinthians 6:1–3

The issue of eternal life in heaven or eternal torment in hell is not a joke. Nor is it a fairy tale, as so many movies would deceive us into concluding. Jesus confirms in His Word that both places exist and are real and eternal. Why would anyone choose not to believe what Jesus says about this extremely serious matter of eternal life or eternal torment when what He has said is the truth?

Imagine this picture in your mind: Someone who deeply loves you comes up to you with two glasses of liquid in their hands. One is labeled "Water = Life." The other is labeled "Poison = Death." The person who loves you presents both glasses to you and urges you to drink the liquid from the glass that is labeled "Water = Life" but knows that he has to leave you to decide which one you will take.

This is a picture of what Jesus is presenting to us. God loves us *so* much that He sent His Son, Jesus Christ, to present to all mankind the way to eternal life (see John 3:16–18, NIV). At the same time as showing us the way to eternal life, He also shows us the opposite; the way that leads to spiritual death and eternal torment in hell. But the decision lies with each individual.

It is futile to try to find God in any other way than the way He has made available to us through the cross of Christ and faith in Him. It is futile to try to get into the kingdom of God by taking a different path than the one Jesus has clearly told us is the only way to get into the kingdom of heaven. The path to eternal life is not the wide, easy, and pleasant path of the multitude of "spiritual" choices that are available today, like some sort of pick and mix candy shop where you can make up your own "bag" of spirituality to suit your personal preferences. Taking these paths may feel nice for us while we are alive but will lead to spiritual death (Prov. 14:12). The path to the kingdom of heaven is straight and narrow. It demands faith, courage, obedience, submission, confession, repentance, diligence, and discipleship in order to remain on the path to heaven.

Let's make this very clear. God does not send anyone to hell. Whoever ends up in hell will arrive there through their own deliberate refusal to believe in the message of salvation through faith in Jesus Christ as the Son of God. The same applies to those who once believed but then abandoned their faith completely and immersed themselves back into sinful, rebellious, disobedient, and unbelieving lifestyles. According to the Word of God, disobedient and rebellious Christians are also deemed to be unbelievers.

I will include some scriptures further in this chapter to confirm this truth. It is not my intention to expound on these scriptures. I will simply list them and allow the Holy Spirit to do His work of convicting of sin and unrighteousness. If an unbeliever or backslidden Christian is then convicted through the reading of the scriptures, they are then in the right position to confess their sins to God and repent of them and turn to God for cleansing, forgiveness, healing, and reconciliation. There is a prayer for unbelievers in appendix A towards the back of this book. I encourage you to read the section and to pray to the Lord with reverential fear and trembling.

Nothing but faith in Jesus Christ will save you from spending eternity in hell. The words of Jesus Himself are irrefutable on this very serious matter. So let us now see what Jesus has to say about the eternal destiny of all who are unbelievers.

> He is ready to separate the chaff from the wheat with his winnowing fork. Then he will clean up the threshing area, gathering the wheat into his barn but burning the chaff with never-ending fire.
>
> —MATTHEW 3:12

> You can enter God's Kingdom only through the narrow gate. The highway to hell is broad, and its gate is wide for the many who choose that way.
>
> —MATTHEW 7:13

> And you will perish, too, unless you repent of your sins and turn to God.
>
> —LUKE 13:3

> And anyone who believes in God's Son has eternal life. Anyone who doesn't obey the Son will never experience eternal life but remains under God's angry judgment.
>
> —JOHN 3:36

> And I assure you that the time is coming, indeed it's here now, when the dead will hear my voice—the voice of the Son of God. And those who listen will live. The Father has life in himself, and he has granted that same life-giving power to his Son. And he has given him authority to judge everyone because he is the Son of Man. Don't be so surprised! Indeed, the time is coming when all the dead in their graves will hear the voice of God's Son, and they will rise again. Those who have done good will rise to experience eternal life, and those who have continued in evil will rise to experience judgment.
>
> —JOHN 5:25–29

Jesus continued, "You are from below; I am from above. You belong to this world; I do not. That is why I said that you will die in your sins; for unless you believe that I Am who I claim to be, you will die in your sins.

—John 8:23–24

But cowards, unbelievers, the corrupt, murderers, the immoral, those who practice witchcraft, idol worshipers, and all liars—their fate is in the fiery lake of burning sulfur. This is the second death.

—Revelation 21:8

Outside the city are the dogs—the sorcerers, the sexually immoral, the murderers, the idol worshipers, and all who love to live a lie.

—Revelation 22:15

The following are a few verses from the apostles in the letters of the New Testament:

Don't be misled—you cannot mock the justice of God. You will always harvest what you plant. Those who live only to satisfy their own sinful nature will harvest decay and death from that sinful nature. But those who live to please the Spirit will harvest everlasting life from the Spirit.

—Galatians 6:7–8

Now concerning how and when all this will happen, dear brothers and sisters, we don't really need to write you. For you know quite well that the day of the Lord's return will come unexpectedly, like a thief in the night. When people are saying, "Everything is peaceful and secure," then disaster will fall on them as suddenly as a pregnant woman's labor pains begin. And there will be no escape.

—1 Thessalonians 5:1–3

Dear friends, if we deliberately continue sinning after we have received knowledge of the truth, there is no longer any sacrifice that will cover these sins. There is only the terrible expectation of God's judgment and the raging fire that will consume his enemies. For anyone who refused to obey the law of Moses was put to death without mercy on the testimony of two or three witnesses. Just think how much worse the punishment will be for those who have trampled on the Son of God, and have treated the blood of the covenant, which made us holy, as if it were common and unholy, and have insulted and disdained the Holy Spirit who brings God's mercy to us.

—HEBREWS 10:26–29

Be careful that you do not refuse to listen to the One who is speaking. For if the people of Israel did not escape when they refused to listen to Moses, the earthly messenger, we will certainly not escape if we reject the One who speaks to us from heaven!

—HEBREWS 12:25

For the time has come for judgment, and it must begin with God's household. And if judgment begins with us, what terrible fate awaits those who have never obeyed God's Good News.

—1 PETER 4:17

So there it is. Scripture tells us that Jesus and the Father are one (John 10:30). Jesus speaks the Word of God. Dare any of us argue with God, the One who has created us? "What sorrow awaits those who argue with their Creator" (Isa. 45:9a).

Despite all the warnings, God still gives all mankind the free will *not* to believe. But if we choose not to believe, then we do this knowing the full and dire consequences of our choice. No one can say that God has not warned us. No one can say that God has sent or will send anyone to hell. It is our unwillingness to yield to the truth and not to believe the message of salvation through faith in Jesus Christ that will cause us to find ourselves in hell.

When a parent tries to lovingly warn their child not to take drugs or consume vast quantities of alcohol and informs them of the devastating consequences that will occur if they do not heed the warnings, the child has a choice to make—heed the warnings and obey or resist the warnings and rebel. If they choose the latter and end up a wreck, they have ended up this way because of *their* choice not to yield to the wise instruction of their parent. The parent did not push the child into the decision to rebel, and the parent also did not bring the devastating consequences upon their child. The consequences are already there as part of the godly, eternal law of reaping what you sow (see Galatians 6:8). The parent warned the child of the devastating consequences of unbelief and rebellion in the same way that God warns all unbelievers of the devastating eternal consequences that await them if they continue to refuse to believe.

So often I have heard unbelievers say, "I will never believe in a God who sends people to hell." The scriptures make it very clear that God does not send anyone to hell. As we will recall, the satanic disposition of sin entered the human race the moment Adam and Eve listened to and believed Satan's deception that they would "not surely die" if they ate the forbidden fruit (see Genesis 3). The moment they ate it, the whole of mankind's eternal destiny was changed from heaven to hell—*not* because God wanted this for them but because sin had entered their disposition and nothing sinful can exist in the kingdom of heaven.

Our only hope of escape from this catastrophic dilemma is to receive the "antidote" of the atoning blood of Jesus Christ that was shed for the remission of the sins of the whole world. However, if we fail to believe this truth and fail to put our faith in Jesus Christ to save us, it is our *own* refusal to believe in Him that will cause us to end up in hell. But even when this is pointed out, many still resist and reject the truth that is revealed to them and still refuse to believe, and they will have to bear the eternal consequences. I realize that I have repeated this frequently, but I have done so to drive home the truth. If you are an unbeliever, I urge you to open your eyes, your ears, and your heart to the only One who can save you and give you eternal life. Jesus Christ is His name.

I deeply encourage you to read appendix A and pray the prayer for unbelievers contained in that section. Let it cause you to fall to your knees before God and pray it out loud from the depths of your soul. The Lord will hear the prayer of a genuinely repentant person, and He will answer your prayer to be saved by putting your faith in His Son, Jesus Christ, as your Lord and Savior.

This decision is so serious; it truly is a matter of life or death eternally. I urge you not to put it off any longer. None of us know when we will draw our last breath. Today may even be our last day on earth. Our life could be cut short way ahead of the "ripe old age" that we hope for. If we have not turned to Jesus Christ to save us prior to our last breath, there will be no opportunity to do so after we have died.

What I have written in this chapter is the truth of the Word of God. It is not my word; it is His. I urge you to study it for yourself and let His truth convict you into confession and repentance of your sins before God.

Your eternal destiny hangs in the balance of the decision that you make and the action that you take. If you are an unbeliever, here are a few questions you could ask yourself to try to find out the root of your unbelief.

- Why am I afraid to believe in Jesus Christ?

- What am I afraid will happen if I believe?

- Why would I prefer to risk ending up in hell rather than believe in Jesus and receive eternal life in heaven when I die?

- Who or what has turned me away from believing in God?

- Why do I continue to allow those events that caused me not to believe to remain unchallenged and not dealt with?

Whatever you discover, only turning to God will bring an end to your unbelief. If you seriously want to turn to God and put your faith and trust in Him now instead of the futility of what the "shifting sands" of this world have to offer, I encourage you to continue reading to the end of this book and then return to appendix A and humble yourself before the Lord in genuine repentant prayer. I am already praying for your salvation.

EPILOGUE

HAVING STUDIED IN detail what Jesus has to say about the end of the world in the Gospels and the Book of Revelation together with the accounts of the apostles and the Old Testament prophets, do we now believe that at some point in time the end of the world will be a reality? Could it even occur in our own lifetime if the Lord commands it? Do we now believe that it is high time we got our lives in order and made ourselves ready for Jesus' return? If we are an unbeliever, does the Word of God on this critical matter of the end of the world cause us to move from a place of unbelief to a place where we seriously begin to grasp the fact that the end of the world will be a reality and that it is not just some manmade story used as the basis for many multimillion dollar games and blockbuster movies?

I am greatly concerned that millions of people are addicted to "end of the world" games and movies but actually dismiss the reality of it when challenged with the truth from God's Word.

If we are an unbeliever, what are we going to do when the end of the world suddenly explodes into a reality when we are not expecting it and we find ourselves in the place of eternal torment—this place that we stubbornly refuse to accept or believe exists? When we find ourselves in hell, there will be nothing that we can do about it, as our eternal destiny will be unchangeable at that catastrophic moment.

If we are a believer living a complacent and halfhearted life in Christ, absorbed in our own little world, oblivious to the escalating signs all around us, we need to wake up urgently and shake off the blinders that Satan has put over our eyes to cause us to drift into a life of compromise. We need to confess our sin of being lukewarm, repent of it, and begin to take back the territory that Satan has stolen from us. We need to start seeing every area of our lives with the "eyes of Christ" and examine our own lives before God and put our lives right with Him before we die or before Jesus returns.

What Jesus has to say about the end of the world is so serious that I actually want to say, "How dare we ignore it?" Finally, here is a straightforward scriptural summary of the truth concerning all that we have read about the eternal destiny of mankind at the end of the world.

If you are a true believer with a repentant heart and lifestyle that is befitting one who believes, the scriptures say you will be raised up to meet the Lord in the air and to live with Him for eternity in heaven. But receive this truth humbly and reverently, mindful of the scripture that says, "Let him that thinketh he standeth take heed lest he fall" (1 Cor. 10:12, KJV). Even the apostle Paul realized that it was possible to end up as a castaway at the final outcome (1 Cor. 9:27, KJV).

If you are a lukewarm, halfhearted believer with one foot in the Lord and the other foot in the world, the scriptures say that when the Lord returns it is highly possible that you will not be permitted entry into the kingdom of heaven if you have not repented of the sins you are allowing to remain in your life. At the Lord's return, should you survive the experience physically, rather than be raised up to meet the Lord in the air, you could find yourself left behind on the earth to endure the horrors of the Tribulation. (See chapter 3 of this book for detail.)

This will be the most horrendous period of suffering the whole earth will face. During this time the scriptures do indicate that there will be time to repent, but it is also made clear that despite the distress of the Tribulation, many will still curse God and refuse to repent (see Revelation 16:9, 11). So wouldn't it be wiser to repent now rather than play Russian roulette with your eternal destiny?

If you should find yourself left behind to face the horrors of the

Tribulation, this period will be your last chance to repent and turn back to Christ before God brings in the final end of the world. If you do not repent, you may find yourself facing the second death—being thrown into the lake of fire (Rev. 20:14). But if you do repent and overcome, the Lord is faithful and just and will forgive you of your sins and cleanse you from all unrighteousness (1 John 1:9). Those whose sins He has forgiven, through their confession and repentance, are the ones whose names are written in the Book of Life. The second death (lake of fire) is for those who have *not* confessed and repented of their sins. Their names will not be found in the Book of Life (Rev. 20:15).

But why would we want to play games with our eternal destiny on the possibility that we might get the chance to repent during the Tribulation? This is utter madness. We might die on the spot when Jesus returns; and if we are still playing games with our faith at that moment, we could be cast into hell. If you should find that you have not been "raptured" and are left behind on the earth to face the tribulation period, *do not* receive the mark of the beast as described in Revelation 13:16–17.

If you do receive it, the scriptures are very clear that your eternal destiny will be in hell forever. If the choice you face during the Tribulation is to take the mark of the beast and remain alive on earth but knowing that when you die you will spend eternity in hell, or to refuse the mark of the beast and be put to death, then *refuse* to take the mark of the beast. Scripture says that those who are martyred for their faith are blessed and will enter the kingdom of heaven in the first resurrection (see Revelation 20:4–6).

Scripture also says that those who come out of the Tribulation will be clothed in white because they will have overcome the devil by the Blood of the Lamb and the word of their testimony (see Revelation 7:9–14). Scripture further says that the souls of those who, before the tribulation, have already been martyred for their faith in Jesus Christ are crying out to the Lord, asking how much longer it will be. The Lord's reply is that it will be when the final number of all those who have *yet* to be martyred have joined them (Rev. 6:11). Therefore, this indicates that many who become believers during the Tribulation will be martyred during this time, possibly for refusing to take the mark of the beast.

Being left behind to face the Tribulation is not something that anyone who professes to be a believer should want to experience. We should be yearning to be raised up at Jesus' appearing and be living our lives in Christ in a manner that befits someone who is a faithful and obedient follower of the King of kings and Lord of lords. However, it is also possible that, when the Lord returns, many backslidden, unrepentant, and halfhearted believers could actually die at the moment of His return. Scripture soberly warns us that such believers will not be permitted to enter the kingdom of heaven. They may be left outside the gates, roaming around naked and ashamed (Rev. 16:15), or they will be cast into hell along with all those who have refused to believe in Jesus Christ (see Revelation 22:12–15). Either way, any place that is not inside the gates of heaven is actually in hell, whether it is just outside the gates of heaven or in the deepest parts of hell. Any place that is *not* inside the gates of heaven we can be certain *is* all a part of hell.

If you are a total unbeliever—remaining so at the Lord's appearing—and if you survive that event, you too will have to go through the Tribulation. The scriptures in the Book of Revelation indicate that there is the possibility of repenting and turning to Christ to save you before the final end of the world comes. But as these scriptures show, despite the horrors of the Tribulation, still the people will refuse to repent of their sins and turn to God (see Revelation 9:20–21; 16:9). If you still refuse to repent during the Tribulation, when the final end comes you will be cast into the lake of fire to join Satan and his demons, the beast and the false prophet, and every other unbeliever (see Revelation 20:10–15).

However, if you are an unbeliever and you *do not* survive the Lord's return, the scriptures say that you will find yourself in hell to face eternal torment. This will continue until the Lord brings in the final end of the world, when those who are in hell will be cast into the eternal lake of fire (see Revelation 20:11–15).

If you are an unbeliever, I urge you to confess your sins *now* before the Tribulation. If you fail to do this, then it will be critical to repent during the Tribulation and not take the mark of the beast.

I ask myself, why anyone would choose to take such catastrophic risks with their eternal destiny? Most people, if you asked them, hope or even think they will go to heaven when they die whether they believe in Jesus Christ or not. The basis they use for this thinking is that they have lived a relatively moral life in comparison to people they see on the daily news reports. Satan has managed to deceive the whole world with this lie, including many believers.

This is not the measure that God uses to determine whether you will enter the kingdom of heaven. The Word of God is very clear on this extremely serious matter, and it is up to us to believe what He says and do something about it before it is too late. If we reject it, we will have to suffer the eternal consequences.

As I finish this book, I pray with the utmost sincerity for the salvation of every man, woman, and child on the face of the earth—from the least to the greatest. I pray for the salvation of every king, queen, prince, and princess; every president, prime minister and every person in positions of government throughout the world; every leader of every nation, city, town, village, street, house, and place of work. I pray that the Holy Spirit will reveal to every person on this earth, whoever they are, that Jesus Christ is Lord—that Jesus Christ is the Messiah. I pray that He will open their spiritual eyes to see that, in God's eyes, if we do not belong to Christ through faith in Him, we are sinners; and unless we confess and repent of our sins, we will find that our eternal destiny will be in hell, regardless of what our minds justify and convince us into believing.

No matter who we are and no matter what position of hierarchy or authority we hold in this earthly life, this does not guarantee us automatic entry into heaven. The truth is that without real, obedient faith in Jesus Christ, we will not be permitted into the kingdom of heaven. No matter how much this truth hurts to hear and take in, it is the truth of the Word of God. This truth will not change just because we don't like hearing it. It is God's truth and He wants us all to face the truth, accept the truth, and humble ourselves before Him in confession and repentance of our sins.

Jesus is the Way, the Truth, and the Life. No man can come to the Father except through Jesus (John 14:6). No other god or self-exalted savior can save us from eternity in hell, even though the doctrines of these gods will deceive us into believing that they are able to. *Nothing else* and *no one* else can save us when the great and terrible Day of the Lord arrives. So, who or what god or "idol" are you worshiping? Who or what are you looking to and trusting in to save you when that time comes?

The reality is, to be certain of entering the kingdom of heaven we must take hold of the message of salvation *now*. We must do something about it *now*. We must confess and repent of our sins *now*. We must obey the Word of God and live our lives in the light of His Word *now*.

Ryle, in the conclusion of the message of his book says,

> And now, reader, in concluding this address, let me ask you, "Whose child are you?" Are you the child of nature or the child of grace? Are you the child of the devil or the child of God? You cannot be both at once. Which are you? Settle the question, reader, for you must die at the last either one or the other. Settle it, reader, for it can be settled, and it is folly to leave it doubtful. Settle it, for time is short, the world is getting old, and you are fast drawing near to the judgment seat of Christ. Settle it, for death is nigh, the Lord is at hand, and who can tell what a day might bring forth? Oh, that you would never rest till the question is settled! Oh, that you may

never feel satisfied till you can say "I have been born again; I am a son of God."[1]

Jesus Christ *will* return, at an appointed time.
Are you ready?

The end of the world will also come, at an appointed time.
Are you ready?

As we come to the end of this book, I will leave you with a final quote from Michael L. Brown,

> And so, everything we do in this world should ultimately be done in anticipation of that day when we will see Him face-to-face. That's really the purpose of it all. Do you live to see Him express approval to you when your eyes first meet? How glorious it will be to see Him smile! There could be no joy possible and no greater satisfaction imaginable. In that indescribable moment—the moment to end all moments—all the pain, all the suffering, all the disappointment, all the hardship, all the labor, all the agony, all the questions will fade into oblivion—when we see the Savior's face. And that is what we must keep in mind every day of our lives. Soon we are going to meet the Lord in person, and we should be getting ready for that moment every hour that we breathe.[2]

One day there will be a shout from heaven saying, "Behold, the Bridegroom cometh!" (Matt. 25:6, kjv). What a glorious day that will be for the bride of Christ! But will the Bridegroom find us all ready at His appearing? He is coming to take back with Him only those who have made themselves ready for Him. Those who are *not* ready He will leave behind. This is the Word of the Lord.

Are we ready?

Are *you* ready?

For in just a very little while, he who is coming will come,
and will not delay.

—HEBREWS 10:37, NIV

Look, I am coming soon!

—REVELATION 22:12

Yes, I am coming soon!

—REVELATION 22:20

Amen! Come, Lord Jesus!

—REVELATION 22:20

I would like to encourage every person who has read this book to this point to continue reading the following poems and all the appendices, as they contain vital messages which I believe the Lord wants us to know.

POEMS BY MICHELE NEAL

(All copyrights 2013 by Michele Neal)

THE CHOSEN ONES

You have been called, but will you be chosen,
When Jesus returns through the sky?
Is your wedding robe on? Is His praise on your tongue?
Will He choose you, or just pass you by?

Do you keep watch? Is your lantern topped up?
Do you shine forth His glorious light?
Or, when you face Him will your lantern grow dim
When He comes like a thief in the night?

Are your feet on the Rock? Are they steadfast and sure
In the wonderful ways of the Lord?
Are you spotless and white? Are you pure in His sight?
Are you daily applying His Word?

You have been called, but will you be chosen
When the final trumpet shall sound?
God shows us the way; will you trust and obey
To make sure you're not left on the ground?

WATCHING AND WAITING

What will you do when Jesus returns?
Will you be ready, my friend?
Will you be watching and waiting for Him?
All the signs point to the end.
Will you sing praises with joy in your heart,
Or will you just hide from His face?
It's all up to you, for you know what to do
To be sure that you'll finish this race.

Was your light shining when someone you knew
Was lost in despair and in strife?
Did you do all that the Lord asked you to,
To guide them to eternal life?
Did you give shelter to someone in need?
Did you give help to the poor?
You know what to do to be sure you'll get through
When Jesus is there "at the door."

Remember how Jesus died there on the cross
To cleanse you from all of your sin!
Remember the day that the Lord changed your life
And gave you His Spirit within!
Use what the Lord gave you, day after day;
Be sure that no chance passes by,
To pray for the sick, then believe that the Lord
Will heal them in front of your eyes!

Jesus will come, and it may not be long,
Returning to take home His bride.
Keep your lamp burning and watch for the signs,
He'll come when we least realize.
The trumpet will sound and a shout will go out,
The Bridegroom is coming at last!
Make sure you are ready; don't leave it too late,
In the blink of an eye it'll be past!

Watching and waiting for Jesus our Lord;
Watching and waiting for Him.
Heeding His warnings, obeying His Word
To be certain that we'll enter in!

One Day Very Soon

One day very soon it's going to be too late,
The Lord is coming back, His "sheep" to separate.

If you do not walk the path that's narrow and straight,
You may find yourself the wrong side of the gate.

One day very soon you'll see before your eyes,
The Lord return in glory, bursting through the skies!
You will know for sure we preached the truth, not lies
When you see God's faithful ones begin to rise!

One day very soon you'll hear the trumpet sound.
There'll be no excuse if you're left on the ground.
Obey the Word of God, therein the truth is found.
You will then rejoice when we are heaven bound!

One day very soon it's going to be too late.
One day very soon the Lord will *shut the gate*!
No more excuses, Jesus will *not* wait.
One day very soon it's going to be *too late*.

A PROPHET HAS NO HONOUR

I tell them of the gospel,
Yet they refuse to understand.
They refuse to see or hear the things
That Jesus has in hand.

Their lives collapse around them;
Distress and anguish reign,
But still they do not want to know
That God can heal their pain.

God's Spirit grieves within me
Each time they turn away;
Rejecting Jesus Christ the Lord,
The Truth, the Life, the Way.

I know His light is shining,
But they will not lift their eyes;

Content to dwell in darkness
And deceive themselves with lies.

They tell me not to speak of Him,
The One who gave me life.
Yet for His name I suffer,
Though it pierces like a knife.

But Jesus counts me worthy,
So I rejoice to suffer shame,
For being chosen of the Lord;
A witness to His name.

I cannot help but speak the things
That I have seen and heard,
Yet still they hearken not to God,
Resisting every Word.

Will their eyes be opened?
Will they ever see?
Will they ever understand
His blood can set them free?

A prophet has no honor
With those who know his name.
They think of him as "one of them"
And reject what he proclaims.

But the prophet is compelled
To speak of all that Jesus taught.
The Day of Judgment hastens,
And our time is running short.

The prophet truly loves you,
Though his message brings much gloom.
He speaks from great compassion,
For he knows that man is doomed.

That's why his words are forceful,
He must shout God's Word abroad,
That salvation is through no one else
But Jesus Christ the Lord!

WILL YOU BELIEVE?

Jesus is the Son of God,
Our lives He came to save.
His broken body on the cross,
His life He freely gave.

A crown of thorns and nail-pierced hands,
A spear thrust in His side;
What sacrifice of love is this,
Who shed His blood and died?

His broken body and His blood,
The Father's gift of love,
Poured out in mercy, forgiveness, and grace,
Flow down from heaven above.

A cold, dark tomb, His resting place;
The end? *No!* It was the start
Of God's great love for all mankind
With wounds that broke His heart.

The tomb could not contain such love;
Its power burst forth with might.
Jesus rose up from the grave
In glorious shining light!

With death defeated on the cross,
He opened up the way
And broke the chains that held us bound
In sin—no debt to pay!

The debt we owe for all we've done
Was paid on Calvary.
The cup of suffering Jesus bore
So we can now walk free!

If someone gave their life for us,
Their love we'd not deny.
We'd live our life a brand new way;
We'd love them 'til we die.

Jesus gave *His* life for *us*!
Why live our lives deceived?
Jesus will reveal the Truth
The moment we believe.

The choice is ours; will we believe?
Heaven waits with bated breath.
The choice we make decides our end
Eternal life, or death.

The message of the cross is this:
Believe and be set free!
Jesus is the Way, the Truth,
The Life eternally!

Appendix A
PRAYER FOR UNBELIEVERS

I WOULD LIKE TO encourage church leaders to read this section too because it is my hope that it may help in reaching those who are unbelievers. While I fully appreciate that many churches are doing a very good and thorough job when unbelievers turn to Christ for salvation, it is equally true that when unbelievers finally come to the place where they know their need of Jesus, there are some leaders who often get them to repeat a hurried prayer to confess and repent of their sins and to ask the Lord's forgiveness. I have witnessed this far too often and it has deeply troubled me.

Granted, all the "essentials" are usually in the prayer that the leader asks the unbeliever to repeat, but I have been troubled at the speed at which it has been done. It often feels as though the leader has another agenda more pressing to him than the life changing situation of the unbeliever that is standing in front of him.

I respectfully say this to all leaders: I am afraid that sinners don't normally turn up to confess and repent of their sins at times that conveniently fit in with our church services. Often they will suddenly be convicted by the Holy Spirit to come forward to give their lives to Christ when we least expect it, and this could be at the precise moment when we want to lock up the building and go home.

As leaders, are we going to rush them through such a life changing moment just so that we can get home for our dinner or make it to the golf course on time? When the lost finally have the conviction and the courage to admit and confess that they are sinners desperately in need of a Savior, we need to demonstrate our joy and excitement by abandoning our schedule to give the sinner the time and the commitment that is essential in order for them to be led to Christ properly. It ought to be done in such a way that the person will know that it is the most important moment of their life as they are led from darkness to light. If they can sense that the leader is agitated or hurrying through the prayer so that he can get home, this poor sinner may never enter the church again; or worse still, he or she may remain lost forever due to the church's insensitive handling.

The moment a sinner says that he or she wants to find Jesus is so serious and so important that I imagine that the entire heavenly host rejoices and worships God as the sinner begins to confess and repent of their sins. (See Luke 15:7, 10.) Jesus died and shed His blood for all mankind. So when a sinner finds the courage to declare that they want to give their life to Jesus, our personal agenda should not become more important than their salvation! I have heard far too many hurried "sinner's prayers" uttered at such a pace that even I as a believer struggled to keep pace with what I was hearing. How can we possibly expect an unbeliever to grasp what it is they are being asked to repeat when it is done in such a rush?

Unbelievers need to be instructed from God's Word what it means to be a sinner, what it means to confess and repent of sin, and what it means to renounce all involvement with our sins. Unbelievers need to be instructed on why they need to ask the Lord to forgive and cleanse them and the importance of believing that they have received His forgiveness. They also need to be instructed on the critical issue of "go and sin no more" (John 8:11).

Throughout my years as a Christian, the lack of corporate and individual instruction that I have observed in many churches of varying denominations has troubled me immensely. I often feel a "righteous anger" rise up inside me that this issue is often being neglected.

For some reason it appears that leaders are afraid to draw attention to the issue of sin; therefore, they feel it unnecessary to hold special teaching sessions on it. The new believer who has just given their life to Christ then has to somehow try to work out why they are still struggling with the temptation to do the things they were doing only days before they turned to Jesus. The church needs to teach them that after confessing and repenting of their sins, it is very likely that they will experience attacks from Satan tempting them to go back to their sins again. They need to be taught that they need to resist the devil and command him to flee in Jesus' name. They need godly teaching to live their lives in obedience to the Word of God in the Holy Bible, with the exhortation from Jesus, "Go now and leave your life of sin" (John 8:11, NIV). This scripture is within the context of the story of the woman caught in the act of adultery, where Jesus forgave her and also did not condemn her but told her to stop sinning. Concerning this story, Michael L. Brown writes,

> Here is a sinner standing guilty before God, and yet she is not condemned. A woman is caught in a blatant violation of her marital covenant committing an act hated by the Lord, yet she is forgiven on the spot. What an example of mercy triumphing over judgment (see James 2:13). But the story doesn't end there. Jesus also gave this woman a solemn charge: "Go and sin no more." In other words, "Leave your adulterous ways behind and live in purity the rest of your days. I forgive your disobedience, but from here on you must be obedient. The time for sinning is over." Yes, God's mercy comes with a mandate. His compassion is coupled with a stern command.[1]

Wow! Well said! But it would seem that this has been neglected so much over the past fifteen years or maybe longer. Is it any wonder that our churches are full of long-standing believers who are still struggling with unconfessed and unrepentant sin? It's as if we are afraid to admit it to anyone. We silently say to ourselves, "I can't tell anyone what I am caught up in! What on earth will they think of me? I must keep the lid on this. No one must find out."

I wrote my book *Come on Church! Wake Up!* following a revelation from the Lord about the need for individual believers and the church as a whole to wake up out of its slumber and deal with unconfessed and unrepentant sin that has been allowed to take root and fester in our lives and our churches. For further reading on this subject please refer to the books that I have listed in the recommended reading section.

Leaders have an immense responsibility before God, particularly when an unbeliever wants to turn to Christ for salvation. The sinner needs to know how serious this moment is; and quite frankly, I don't believe that asking them to repeat a hasty one-minute sinner's prayer is adequate. A serious and deeply meaningful prayer from the heart is what is needed. It should be spoken out loud to the Lord from a place of brokenness and sorrow and a heart that has been convicted that without Christ it is heading for eternity in hell.

I have written the following prayer that could be used. If you prefer you could pray something similar that the Lord may lay upon your heart. If you are an unbeliever and know that you need to turn to Jesus for your salvation, I urge you to take this opportunity *now* and pray this prayer.

PRAYER

Lord God, I do not know You, but this day I declare that I want to know You. I confess that I have continually resisted You and refused to believe in You and have made excuses to reject You for my own selfish reasons.

This day I want to mark as the first day of the rest of my life—the day that I cross over the line from unbelief to belief. I have refused to believe that I am a sinner in need of salvation, but this day I want to yield to Your truth and put my faith in Jesus Christ to save me.

Today (insert date) I confess before You all of my sins (make a list of all the sins you are knowingly involved in and declare them out loud to the Lord) and ask You, Lord, to cleanse me from all of my sins and to forgive me.

I confess with my mouth and believe in my heart the truth that Jesus Christ died on the cross and shed His blood for my sins. Because I accept and believe that this awesome sacrifice of love actually took place for all mankind and I put my faith in the One who bore the punishment for all my sins on the cross—Jesus Christ Your precious Son, I can come to You, confess my sins, repent of them, and receive Your forgiveness, healing, and restoration. I believe at that moment my life is made new in Jesus Christ and my old sins are washed away because of the shed blood of Jesus.

Thank You for this amazing sacrifice, Lord. I am truly sorry that I have spent my life refusing to accept this most precious free gift. I am truly sorry that I have spent so much of my life in sinful ways, stubbornly upholding my "right" to live my life however I pleased.

I now make this commitment to turn away from my old life this day, Lord, and I turn to You. I want Jesus to be my Lord and Savior. Fill my heart with a hunger and thirst to read Your Word and fill me with Your Holy Spirit so that I can understand Your Word, obey it, and apply it to my daily life.

I want to obey Your Word to follow Jesus' example to be baptized by full immersion in water as a symbol of the washing away of my old life (see Matthew 3:13–15). I want to receive the promise made by Jesus of the power of the Holy Spirit (see Acts 1:8) by receiving the baptism of the Holy Spirit in the same way that the disciples did on the day of Pentecost, so that You can use me to be a witness for Jesus wherever You send me (see Acts 2:1–4).

I give my life to You, Lord, and I ask You to use my life for Your glory. Help me to remain humble so that I do not boast that the works You do in and through me are of my own strength or ability. Let me always give You the glory and the praise for whatever You choose to do through this broken vessel that I am. Thank You that You take flawed and broken vessels and make them new when we put our faith in Jesus Christ.

I accept the truth that I will make mistakes in my new life in Christ. Convict me each time that I do mess up so that I can come to You quickly to confess and repent of whatever sins I have allowed into my life and receive Your cleansing, forgiveness, and restoration.

Lead me, Lord, to the place that You want me to have fellowship with other believers where I will receive wholesome, godly teaching based on the entirety of Your holy Word, without compromise. Keep me grounded in the truth of Your Word so that I remain strong and immoveable in my faith in Jesus Christ and will live my life in obedience to Your Word.

I want to be ready when the Lord Jesus Christ returns so that I will be counted among those who will inherit eternal life and will enter into Your glorious kingdom on that awesome day.

Thank You, Lord. Thank You, my heavenly Father, for accepting me now as Your beloved child through my faith in Jesus Christ.

I pray this sincerely, in Jesus' name. Amen.

Now that you have prayed this prayer, I strongly urge you to remove yourself from every situation that is part of your previous sinful lifestyle. God has seen you pray and has heard your prayer. Now you have a big part to play in living your life in ways that honor and please the Lord, in ways that are in keeping with someone who professes to be a follower of Christ.

It would be wrong of me to say that you will not slip up, because it is highly likely that you will; I have many times. I would say with certainty that all Christians slip up throughout their life in Christ. Any Christian who says that they haven't needs to read the following scripture again: "If we claim to be without sin, we deceive ourselves and the truth is not in us" (1 John 1:8, NIV). The most important thing to remember when we slip up is to do what it says in 1 John 1:9, "If we confess our sins, he is faithful and just to forgive us our sins and purify us from all unrighteousness" (NIV).

I urge you to keep doing that each time you slip up, as it will keep you focused on the Lord and it will help to prevent you from falling back into your sinful life. I have personally found that when I failed to confess my sins to the Lord, I gradually became desensitized to the sins I was committing and no longer felt it was even necessary to confess them. This is a dangerous condition to be in, and so I encourage you to have a commitment of mind and heart that willingly confesses daily sin to the Lord. I have covered this aspect fully in my previous book, *Come on Church! Wake Up!* It was written out of my own painful, personal experience of unconfessed and unrepentant sin in my life as a believer, so you can be reassured of its truthfulness and integrity. I have found that the best and most helpful books are those that have been written from personal experience rather than from mere knowledge that has been taught and learned but without any personal experience.

If you have become a new believer but your church does not seem to be concerned about dealing with sin within the church, I encourage you to go and find a church that does take this issue seriously! Ask the Lord to lead you to the right place.

Pray to the Lord simply, talking to Him openly as you would with a close friend. He is right beside you waiting for you to ask Him for whatever it is that you need. He will even send His angels to help you if necessary, as His Word says that angels are messengers who are sent to minister to those who will inherit salvation (Heb. 1:14). That is awesome! My daughter and I have had the humbling experience of being blessed by several angelic interventions and protection in times of need. Although I haven't got room in this book to give these testimonies, I know that angelic assistance is very real!

However, a word of caution: We are not supposed to directly ask angels to help us. We must call out to *God* to help us. And if He so chooses, He will dispatch His angels to help us. If He does so and we are actually privileged to be aware of such an encounter with a ministering angel, we must be sure to give the glory and thanks to God, not the angels. Angels are just carrying out the will of God, and they do not need or want our thanks for it.

Do not fall into the trap of calling on the angels to help you, because this is contrary to the Word of God. It will cause you to place your trust and faith in them rather than God. Calling on the angels and worshiping angels is the teaching and practice of some alternative "spiritual" organizations, and it is not the will of God. Praying to or calling on the angels for help and guidance can open us up to being visited and assisted by Satan himself and his demons, who are more than happy to deceive people by masquerading as angels of light (2 Cor. 11:14–15).

This is why the Word of God warns us to worship only God. He knows what will happen if we project our focus and our prayers on to other spiritual beings. It will cause us to be led into deception. We will believe we have had holy angelic assistance or guidance but will not realize that it was in fact the fallen angels of Satan or even Satan himself.

In the Book of Revelation, an angel appeared to the apostle John. John fell at the angel's feet as though dead. But the angel rebuked John and told him to stand up on his feet and told him not to worship him, as he was just a servant like John was, and that John was to worship only God. This happened on two separate occasions. (See Revelation 19:10; 22:8–9.)

So, be sure to pray to God and to worship God. Do not get caught in the trap of praying to any of God's created heavenly beings, not even Mary (the mother of Jesus) or any of the apostles. I am aware that some believers do pray to the saints of old who are now dead and kneel before statues of them in their church buildings. This is what God's Word has to say about such religious practices.

> The idols of the nations are merely things of silver and gold, shaped by human hands. They have mouths but cannot speak, and eyes but cannot see. They have ears but cannot hear, and noses but cannot smell. And those who make idols are just like them, as are all who trust in them.
> —Psalm 135:15–18

> What fools they are who carry around their wooden idols and pray to gods that cannot save!
> —Isaiah 45:20b

> What good is an idol carved by man, or a cast image that deceives you? How foolish to trust in your own creation—a god that can't even talk! What sorrow awaits you who say to wooden idols, "Wake up and save us!" To speechless stone images you say, "Rise up and teach us!" Can an idol tell you what to do? They may be overlaid with gold and silver, but they are lifeless inside. But the LORD is in his holy Temple. Let all the earth be silent before him.
> —Habakkuk 2:18–20

> But the people...still refused to repent of their evil deeds and turn to God. They continued to worship demons and idols made of gold, silver, bronze, stone and wood—idols that can neither see nor hear nor walk!
> —Revelation 9:20

God's Word is very stern about engaging in this kind of activity. He does not want us to do this. It can open us up to being deceived by Satan and his demons masquerading as angels of light. We should obey the Word of God and *only* pray to God and worship *only* Him.

So, if you have prayed the prayer above or something similar that the Lord has laid on your heart to pray and are now a new believer, I will be praying for you to be strong in the Lord and to remain rooted in His Word and obedient to all that His Word says concerning your life in Christ.

In John 3:3, Nicodemus, who was a God-fearing man, asked Jesus what he must do to inherit eternal life. Jesus declared, "Very truly I tell you, no one can see the kingdom of God unless they are born again...unless they are born of water and the Spirit" (John 3:3, 5, NIV).

This is very serious! Many churches today are full of people who have a nominal faith but have not been born again. They may be in churches that do not even preach or teach that they must be born again; or they may know about it but feel that it is not what they want and may be quite content to just do their own thing where Christianity is concerned. It is sadly very true to say that many believers have their own version of being a Christian, which excludes much of what Jesus taught. They attend church each week, sing hymns or worship songs, join in the prayers and fellowship with other believers, but resist the message that they must be born again.

They may have never confessed or repented of their sins or feel any need to do so. Some churches do not even preach what repentance is. Repentance means to turn away completely from your old sinful way of life, forsaking all the things you used to do in your life as an unbeliever and then changing your thinking and your actions so that they conform to the Word of God.

I do not believe it would be wrong to say that the church of Jesus Christ, in this present time that we are in, is drowning with the unconfessed and unrepentant sin in people's lives and within the church as a whole. Sin within the church is causing the devastating and catastrophic downfall of leaders, the split of churches, and at times the complete closure of churches. It need not be this way if only the church would heed Jesus' warnings to wake up and make itself ready for His return. (Hence my previous book, *Come on Church! Wake Up!*)

So, dearly beloved new believer, my heart and my prayers go out to you to remain in Christ *to the very end* when Jesus returns. He is coming back to redeem those who are ready at His appearing, those who have remained steadfast and have persevered and overcome all the onslaughts that Satan has thrown at them because of their faith in Jesus Christ as their Lord and Savior.

Do not buckle under Satan's pressure to give up your faith. Immerse yourself in prayer and the reading of God's Word. Hunger and thirst after His Word and consume it eagerly! Do not be tempted to believe the false doctrines of other "spiritual" organizations that preach a different gospel (see Galatians 1:6–9). From over twenty years of personal experience, I can confirm to you that God's Word, as written in the Holy Bible, is the truth, the whole truth, and nothing but the truth.

Mixing God's Word with the false doctrines of other "spiritual" organizations will produce catastrophic results. Here is an analogy. You have just bought the latest top of the line BMW and have got the right manual to help you get the best performance out of it. It is what you turn to when something appears to be wrong in its functioning. You use the manual faithfully for a few years. But after a while you think you know how to get your car functioning properly without needing to refer to the correct book. Something goes wrong with your car "big time"; but instead of reading the correct book, you ask a friend if they have got a manual for their Ford Fiesta that you could have a quick look at to try to sort out the problem with your BMW! While there is nothing wrong with having a Ford Fiesta, trying to fix a BMW's problem using a Fiesta handbook will only produce disaster!

So, applying the above analogy to our Christian lives, we learn that we must not mix the Word of God with any other "beliefs" or "truths" from any other "spiritual" organization. The eternal consequences will be catastrophic for anyone who thinks it is okay to muddy the waters of God's Word.

Being a Christian is a serious matter. The promises that are laid up for us in heaven are immense and beyond our ability to fully imagine. Jesus wants us to receive these, but they are the eternal inheritance of those who have taken their faith and their calling seriously.

As a new believer, you have much to learn. But if you obey the Lord, it will be wonderful and rewarding. At times what the Word of God teaches will be hard to bear. But from my own personal experience I can confirm that it is much better to obey the Word of the Lord when He instructs you and not willfully or stubbornly resist it.

God bless you in your new life in Christ. Remain anchored to the only One who can save you on that day when the end of the world comes.

Who is that One?

Jesus Christ our Lord and Savior!

Halleluiah!

Appendix B
PRAYER FOR BELIEVERS CAUGHT UP IN UNREPENTANT SIN

I F YOU ARE a Christian who is caught up in unconfessed and unrepentant sin I urge you to pray to the Lord the prayer I have written a little later in this section, from the depths of your heart. Whether you are still attending church or have actually left, I do not know what you are struggling with or to what depths you are caught up in sin, but I would like you to know that I, too, have struggled with unrepentant and repetitive sin as a Christian.

God, in His great mercy, has shown me how much He loves me by revealing to me my unconfessed and unrepentant sin and disciplining me to confess it and repent of it. Then I could receive His cleansing, forgiveness, and restoration. That *truly* is the love of God! He could have left me in my sinful mess and abandoned me to the consequences of my sinful choices—eternity in hell. But instead, His incredible love reached down to me in my unconfessed mess. Then He chastened and disciplined me to repent of it all out of His awesome heart of love! This process is extremely painful; but it is equally filled with indescribable grace, forgiveness, freedom, joy, and peace! Praise God!

Stephanie Cottam describes God's mercy, grace and love towards repentant believers like this:

> How awesome to know that He delights in us and wants to know us, but more than that—He wants us to be open and real with Him. To lay aside our masks when we come before Him and openly admit when we mess up. Then He can

> forgive us our sins and cleanse us from all unrighteousness
> (1 John 1:9), preparing us for the Day when He can present us
> cleansed and pure to His Son (2 Corinthians 14:4).[1]

If we truly want to serve the Lord and know that what we are doing, whether secretly or openly, is not in keeping with His holy Word, the Lord *will* reveal our sins to us. He will convict us of our sin and unrighteousness so that we can do something about it. He knows our eternal destiny if we do not heed His warnings. However, God still leaves us with the free will to either heed His warnings or choose not to heed them.

As I have previously mentioned throughout this book, if we refuse to yield to God and obey His Word when He has shown us the way, it is our choice that determines our eternal destiny. God holds open His offer of mercy, forgiveness, and reconciliation to us right up to the moment that we draw our last breath. But after that, there is no more opportunity to repent—only judgment.

So, if you believe in Jesus Christ but have got yourself caught up in sin that you are trying to justify as something that is okay to do and are not accepting and admitting it as sinful, I urge you now to heed God's warnings to do so. It may be the last opportunity that you get, as none of us know when our last breath will be.

Come humbly before the Lord in brokenness and shame for the sins you have allowed yourself to drift in to. Do this with sincerity, wanting to be rid of the habits and lifestyle that have deceived and enticed you away from obedience to the holy Word of God.

God longs for you to spend eternity with Him in heaven. It is His heart's desire that you enter the city gates so that He can say to you, "Well done, my good and faithful servant!" (Matt. 25:23), and, "Come, you who are blessed by my Father; take your inheritance, the kingdom prepared for you since the creation of the world" (v. 34, NIV).

But, as I have shown throughout this book, and particularly in chapter 6, only those believers who live their lives in Christ in obedience to His Word will inherit eternal life. No believer who rejects God's Word on sin will be allowed into the kingdom of heaven.

So, at this critical point you are faced with a choice: (1) yield to God's truth about your continual unrepentant sins and confess and repent of them now, or (2) continue as you are—in rebellion to the Word of God. I urge you to confess and repent now. God's Word is the truth when He says,

> If we claim to be without sin, we deceive ourselves and the truth is not in us. If we confess our sins, he is faithful and just to forgive us our sins and cleanse us from all unrighteousness. *If we claim we have not sinned*, we make Him out to be a liar and His Word has no place in our lives.
> —1 JOHN 1:8–10, NIV, EMPHASIS ADDED

If you know you are a believer and are *making excuses* for your sin, in effect you are claiming that you are not sinning. The above scripture tells us that when we do this, we are deceiving ourselves and the truth is not in us. Effectively we are telling God that He is the one who is lying for telling us that we are sinning, when in fact the truth is *we* are the ones who are the liars. Making excuses for our sins is very serious in the eyes of God.

Yes, this scripture tells us that if we will confess our sins, God is faithful and just to forgive us of our sins and cleanse us from all unrighteousness. But please allow me to strongly warn you that this scripture *does not* give believers a license to continue sinning simply because God's mercy and grace are freely extended to us whereby we can come before Him in confession and repentance of our daily sins. To keep on sinning makes a mockery of the mercy and grace of God. The apostle Paul's letter to the *believers* in Rome confirms clearly that we should not keep on sinning:

> Yes, Adam's one sin brings condemnation for everyone, but Christ's one act of righteousness brings a right relationship

with God and new life for everyone. Because one person disobeyed God, many became sinners. But because one other
person obeyed God, many will be made righteous. God's law
was given so that all people would see how sinful they were.
But as people sinned more and more, God's wonderful grace
became more abundant. So just as sin ruled over all people
and brought them to death, now God's wonderful grace rules
instead, giving us right standing with God and resulting in
eternal life through Jesus Christ our Lord. Well then, should
we keep on sinning so that God can show us more and more
of His wonderful grace? Of course not! Since we have died to
sin, how can we continue to live in it?

—Romans 5:18–6:2

Further, Paul's letter to Titus, who was a believer, also confirms
this:

For the grace of God has appeared that offers salvation to all
men. It teaches us to say "No" to ungodliness and worldly
passions, and to live self-controlled, upright and godly lives
in this present age, while we wait for the blessed hope—the
glorious appearing of our great God and Savior, Jesus Christ,
who gave himself for us to redeem us from all wickedness
and to purify for himself a people that are his very own,
eager to do what is good.

—Titus 2:11–14, NIV

Again, Paul says the same things to the Thessalonian *believers*:

It is God's will that you should be sanctified:...that each of
you should learn to control your own body in a way that is
holy and honorable, not in passionate lust like the pagans,
who do not know God.

—1 Thessalonians 4:3–5, NIV

And again,

For God did not call us to be impure, but to live a holy life. Therefore, anyone who rejects this instruction does not reject a human being but God, who gave you his Holy Spirit.

—1 THESSALONIANS 4:7–8, NIV

To the *believers* in the Ephesian church, Paul writes:

But among you there must not be even a hint of sexual immorality, or of any kind of impurity, or of greed, because these are improper for God's holy people. Nor should there be obscenity, foolish talk or coarse joking, which are out of place, but rather thanksgiving. For of this you can be sure: No immoral, impure or greedy person—such a man is an idolater—has any inheritance in the kingdom of Christ and of God. Let no one deceive you with empty words, for because of such things God's wrath comes on those who are disobedient. Therefore do not be partners with them.

—EPHESIANS 5:3–7, NIV

The Lord God spoke similar words through the prophet Isaiah:

Wash and make yourselves clean. Take your evil deeds out of my sight! Stop doing wrong. Learn to do right.

—ISAIAH 1:16–17A, NIV

And finally, listen to what the Lord told the prophet Jeremiah to speak to His people:

Don't be fooled into thinking that you will never suffer because the Temple is here. It's a lie! Do you really think you can steal, murder, commit adultery, lie, and burn incense to Baal and all those other new gods of yours, and then come here and stand before me in my Temple and chant, "We are safe!"—only to go right back to all those evils again? Don't you yourselves admit that this Temple, which bears my name, has become a den of thieves? Surely I see all the evil going on there. I, the LORD, have spoken!

—JEREMIAH 7:8–11

So if you are a believer caught up in unconfessed and unrepentant sin and you want to get yourself right with God so that you can start living your life in readiness for Jesus' return, I encourage you to pray the following prayer or a similar one as the Holy Spirit leads you.

PRAYER

Father, I come before You with the mess that I have made of my life. At some point I have allowed myself to be deceived and enticed into sinful thoughts and sinful behavior. And I have continually made excuses for these, foolishly believing that I would still inherit eternal life despite being involved in sinful practices of which I have not confessed and repented.

Thank You for loving me so much by revealing to me my unconfessed and unrepentant sin and for showing me the eternal consequences if I continue living in these ungodly ways, even though it is painful.

Father, right now I confess every one of my sins that I am struggling with and am caught up in of which I have not repented. (I suggest that you list all of your unconfessed and unrepentant sins and name them out loud to the Lord in this prayer.)

Lord, I confess out loud to You into the heavenly realms that I have sinned in all these ways and have grieved You by participating in them. I am truly sorry, Lord, and I ask for Your forgiveness and cleansing through the precious blood of Christ.

As of this day (insert date), I renounce all my involvement in these sins; I repent of them and turn back to Christ. I do not want to participate in sinful practices anymore. And I ask You, Lord, to help me, convict me in the future, and use the correcting rod of Your holy Word if I begin to stray again, so that I can quickly come back onto the straight and narrow path that leads to eternal life.

This day I declare before all of heaven that I want to live my life in obedience to the holy Word of God. I want to yield to the Lord's will, to choose to do what is acceptable and pleasing in His sight, and to resist temptation's enticement to fall back into sin again.

Your Word says, "Godly sorrow leads to repentance which leads to salvation" (2 Cor. 7:10, NIV). I confess that I have stubbornly made excuses for my sins and have rejected Your Word that says I need to have godly sorrow about them.

Father, in Your love for me, I ask that You would create in me a heart that is truly sorry, with a godly sorrow, for the sins I have committed while I self-righteously upheld my right to still call myself a believer. Let me know what it means to feel and fully experience the godly sorrow that leads to repentance, which leads to salvation. My heart and my life need a complete transformation; and I know that only You, Lord, are able to do this in me.

I give all that I am to You this day, Father. I am Your prodigal child who has mucked around in the pigsty of the world, but now I have finally come to my senses and am returning back to my Father's house in confession and repentance of my sins. Let me fall into Your loving arms of forgiveness and be fully restored in my relationship with You. (See the story of the Prodigal Son in Luke 15:11–31.)

Thank You, Father, for loving me so much that You have left the gate wide open for Your wayward children to return to You when we stray into sin. This gate is the gate of confession and repentance, which You have mercifully revealed to me and which I humbly accept and acknowledge as the truth in order to receive Your forgiveness, cleansing, and restoration.

Father, please give me a deep hunger and thirst to read and obey Your Word and to no longer compromise with it when faced with temptation to sin. Help me to remain rooted and grounded in the truth of Your Word so that my life will be continually pleasing to You. I want to be diligent and steadfast in reading, obeying, and applying Your Word.

I want to persevere and overcome to the end so that I will hear the words I long to hear; You saying, "Well done, my good and faithful servant!" and, "Come, you who are blessed by my Father, inherit the Kingdom prepared for you from the creation of the world" (Matt. 25:21, 34). This is the most precious possession that anyone could ever inherit, and I truly want to receive it.

I offer this prayer to You, Father, with thanksgiving and faith, in the name of my Lord and Savior Jesus Christ. Amen.

Appendix C
PRAYER OF THANKSGIVING
FOR TRUE BELIEVERS

I FELT IT WOULD be good to include a prayer of thanksgiving to God for all that He has done and continues to do for those who are true believers. So often we forget to give Him the thanks and praise due Him because we are pulled by the pressures and demands of daily life that scream for our attention.

Below is a prayer that you could pray, or you could pray something similar as the Holy Spirit leads you.

PRAYER

Thank You, Lord, that in Your great mercy and love, You have shown me the way of salvation through Your precious holy Word. Thank You that Your Word says that there is no other name by which we can be saved than the name of Jesus Christ (Acts 4:12).

Thank You that You revealed to me my need of salvation by showing me that while I did not believe in the name of Your one and only Son, Jesus Christ, I was a sinner condemned already and destined for eternity in hell (see John 3:16–18). You showed me I needed to confess and repent of all my sins so that I could receive Your cleansing and forgiveness through the shed blood of Jesus Christ in order to be able to receive eternal life. (See Acts 2:38; 1 John 1:9; 2 Corinthians 7:9–10.)

Thank You for showing me from Your Word that I needed to be born again of water and of the Spirit in order to inherit eternal life in the kingdom of God (see John 3:1–8). Thank You for making real to me the need to be baptized in accordance with the way that Jesus showed us in Your holy Word (see Matthew 3:13–15). Thank You for filling me with Your Holy Spirit in fulfillment of Your Word (see Acts 2:1–4).

Thank You that Your Word says I am a new creation in Christ (2 Cor. 5:17, NIV). Help me, Lord, to live my life each day in the power of Your Holy Spirit, walking in the Spirit so that I will not fulfill the lust of the flesh (Gal. 5:16, KJV).

I know that how I live my life in Christ on earth is a major part of my witness and testimony to all those in the world who do not believe in You. In Your power and strength, let my life demonstrate the truth and fulfillment of Your Word. Help me to remain pliable in Your hands, so that I willingly yield in submission and obedience to Your Word in relation to every area of my life.

With all my heart, I want to be raised up on the day when Jesus returns and to enter the gates of heaven and hear You say to me, "Well done, my good and faithful servant," and, "Come, you who are blessed by my Father, inherit the Kingdom prepared for you from the creation of the world" (Matt. 25:21, 34). I cannot begin to imagine all that You have stored up for those who truly love, worship, and follow You (see 1 Corinthians 2:9); but with all my heart I want to receive all that Your Word promises, both in this earthly life and in the eternal life to come.

I do not want to find myself left outside the gates naked and ashamed and in hell because I lived a lukewarm, complacent, and halfhearted life as a Christian in disobedience and rebellion to Your Word (see Revelation

16:15). Search my heart and my life and show me any sin that is there (see Psalm 139:23); let Your Holy Spirit convict me to confess it and repent of it quickly.

I know that I cannot be complacent about my salvation and need to examine my life to see if my faith is genuine (2 Cor. 13:5). Help me to do this daily, and even hourly if need be, so that I do not take the precious shed blood of Jesus for granted. Thank You for the gift of eternal life that is available to all who will believe in Your Son, Jesus Christ (John 3:16) and who obey Him (Heb. 5:9).

Please create in me a willing and obedient heart to live my life knowing that eternal life in the kingdom of heaven is at stake for any believer who does not live their life in readiness for Jesus' return (see Matthew 25:1-13). Help me to accept the seriousness and the truth of Your Word which says, "But small is the gate and narrow is the road that leads to life, and only a few find it" (Matt. 7:14, NIV).

Help me to hold onto Your Word in my heart and worship You in reverential fear and awe of Your holiness (Heb. 12:28, NIV). Help me to not allow the doctrines of man to deceive me into forsaking Your truth for a "different truth" or a "different gospel," which is contrary to Your Word in the Holy Bible (see Galatians 1:6-9).

You are the Rock on which I stand.

You are my Anchor in times of storm.

You are my Strength when I am weak.

Your Word is the lamp that lights my path.

Your love is beyond description.

Your mercy is beyond comprehension.

What love is this that would reach down and save a wretch like me?

It is the unending, overwhelming, indescribable, and unfathomable love of God displayed to us through the broken body and the shed blood of His Son, Jesus Christ, on the cross, to open up the way of salvation for all mankind from every nation, tribe, and tongue on the face of this earth, when they accept the message of the Cross of Christ and put their faith and trust in Jesus as their Lord and Savior!

Thank You, Father, for searching for me and finding me in all my sinfulness, and for transforming my life through my faith in Jesus Christ. Let me never forget what it cost You to set me free from the eternal penalty of sin. Let this fact and reality be seared in the depths of my soul and create in me such a reverential fear of Your holiness and justice that it keeps me walking obediently on the narrow path that leads to eternal life.

I pray this prayer to You, Lord, in the name of Your dear and blessed Son, Jesus Christ. Amen.

RECOMMENDED READING

I BELIEVE THAT THE following books are essential, urgent reading for every believer who wants to be ready for the return of the Bridegroom.

Brown, Michael L. *Go and Sin No More*. Concord, NC: Equal-Time Books, 1999. ISBN: 978-0-615-73019-6.

Byun, Seung Woo. *Christians Going to Hell*. Lake Mary, FL: Creation House, 2006. ISBN: 978-1-59185-871-3.

Cottam, Stephanie. *Ready or Not—He Is Coming*. Saffron Walden, UK: Glory to Glory Publications, 2012. ISBN: 978-0-9567831-5-8.

Jeffrey, Grant R. *The New Temple and the Second Coming*. Colorado Springs: WaterBrook Press, 2007. ISBN 978-1-400071070.

Ryle, J. C. *Are You Ready for the End of Time? Understanding Future Events from Prophetic Passages of the Bible*. Ross-shire, Scotland: Christian Focus Publications, 2001. ISBN: 1-85792-747-8. www.christianfocus.com.

NOTES

CHAPTER 1
THE REASON FOR THIS BOOK

1. Stephanie Cottam, *Ready or Not—He Is Coming* (Saffron Walden, England: Glory to Glory Publications, 2012), 62.
2. Ibid., 63–64.
3. J. C. Ryle, *Are You Ready for the End of Time? Understanding Future Events from Prophetic Passages of the Bible* (Ross-shire, Scotland: Christian Focus Publications, 2001), 33.
4. Ibid., 139.

CHAPTER 2
WHAT JESUS SAID: THE GOSPELS

1. Cottam, 86.
2. Seung Woo Byun, *Christians Going to Hell* (Lake Mary, FL: Creation House, 2006), 279. Used by permission.
3. Cottam, 69.

CHAPTER 3
WHAT JESUS SAID: THE BOOK OF REVELATION

1. Cottam, 120.
2. Ibid., 133.

CHAPTER 5
WHAT THE PROPHETS SAID

1. Cottam, 91.

CHAPTER 6
THE END OF THE WORLD FOR BELIEVERS

1. Ryle, 173.
2. Ibid., 175.
3. Ibid., 38.
4. Byun, 174.
5. Ryle, 13–14.
6. Ibid., 37.
7. Michael L. Brown, *Go and Sin No More* (Concord, NC: EqualTime Books, 1999), 233.
8. Byun, 186.
9. Brown, 96.

10. Ibid., 96–97.
11. Ibid., 99.
12. Ibid., 100.
13. Ibid., 125.

CHAPTER 7
THE END OF THE WORLD FOR UNBELIEVERS

1. Oswald Chambers, *My Utmost for His Highest*, ed. James Reimann (Grand Rapids, MI: Discovery House, 1992), July 24 entry.

EPILOGUE

1. Ryle, 179.
2. Brown, 228.

APPENDIX A
PRAYER FOR UNBELIEVERS

1. Brown, 88.

APPENDIX B
PRAYER FOR BELIEVERS CAUGHT UP IN UNREPENTANT SIN

1. Cottam, 106.

ABOUT THE AUTHOR

ALTHOUGH I WAS born on the Isle of Wight in 1961, I have lived a very nomadic life, having lived in over twenty-five houses in my fifty-two years! Four of those years were spent at a boarding school on the Isle of Wight, and I am so thankful to the Lord that I was able to share those years there with my twin sister, Sharon. We were like "two peas in a pod"! At the age of ten we lived in Gibraltar for about two years, which was a wonderful experience.

Throughout my life, I have believed God existed and I knew that Jesus had died on a cross; but that was as far as my faith went, despite being confirmed into the Anglican Church at boarding school at the age of thirteen and having attended many different churches over the past thirty years.

No one explained to me until 1992 that, in the eyes of God, I was a sinner and was in need of salvation. Once this had been explained to me, the following day I was baptized by full immersion in water and was filled with the Holy Spirit and spoke in tongues, just like the first disciples did on the Day of Pentecost! I was transformed from a broken and depressed wreck into a person full of the joy of the Lord, and I knew that God had done something dramatic inside me through my new faith in Jesus Christ. The Lord has performed many healing miracles in my life and the lives of others who I have prayed for in His authority and in His name.

However, through many wrong choices I have made in my life in Christ, my growth in faith suffered many setbacks over the past twenty-one years. Thankfully, God, in His great mercy, reached down and extended His hand of grace and love to me and has shown me exactly what my unconfessed and unrepentant sins look like in His sight. Such times have been a grueling experience, but the fruit of such pain produced my first book, *Come on Church! Wake Up!*, published in January 2013.

I thank the Lord for the experiences He took me through and is still taking me through each day. My life has become very different. All the things that consumed my life and my time I am no longer interested in anymore. This aspect was a sudden transformation brought about by the Holy Spirit following a revelation from the Lord that the time I spent doing these things was causing me to neglect my daily relationship with Him.

Since that experience in October 2011, my desire to do the things I was doing excessively before has been completely extinguished! The things that were consuming all my time and energy were not sinful in themselves, but my immoderate level of doing them was akin to "idolatry." So God intervened in a big way to get my attention. And while He was at it, God revealed to me some areas of unconfessed and unrepentant sin that needed dealing with. My first book, written for the glory of God, was a result of this. I am now doing things I would never have dreamt or imagined were possible for me to do, but I do all of this now for God and for His glory. This is the only thing that matters to me now.

In-between writing books, I am a housewife and the mother of a beautiful adult daughter, Emma. I enjoy open countryside, reading, photography, and days out at the seaside!

As I close this biography, I would like to share with you God's most recent amazing hand of blessing. By the time you read this paragraph, I will have moved back to the place of my birth—the Isle of Wight. The Lord has made this possible for us. In an instant, He brought about a miraculous situation that we had hoped in our natural minds to achieve in about five years time. One moment our moving there was just a distant dream, and the next moment we were virtually on our way. God is *so* amazing!

But it gets even more amazing! There are small towns and

villages on the Isle of Wight called Sandown, Shanklin, Lake, Ventnor, and Bonchurch. My daughter will not be moving to the island with us, as she will be staying at university in Liverpool to do a master's degree. She is moving into accommodation near to the university, and she has discovered that there are some roads surrounding the street where she will be living, which are called Sandown Lane, Shanklin Road, Lake Road, Ventnor Road, and Bonchurch Drive!

It is possible that one of these road names may exist somewhere in Liverpool, but what are the chances of all five of these Isle of Wight names occurring as road names directly around the place where she will be living, and at precisely the same time that we will be moving to the island? God sure does have a wonderful sense of humor. He has even made sure that she can feel connected to us by arranging for her to live in lodgings that are surrounded by roads that will constantly remind her of where we are.

And finally, here is the "icing on the cake." All my life I have loved the sea and the sound of seagulls. Whenever we go away on holiday, the first thing I long to hear is the sound of the waves rolling up the seashore and the seagulls squawking. I am even known for my imitation of them! We are now living on an island with beaches at almost every turn and seagulls flying overhead everywhere we go. Praise and glory to the Lord!

These little "holy moments" are signs to us that the Lord's hand is guiding our every step. When the Lord takes care of even the most personal details like this, it just makes me love Him more and more! I want to run up to Him and give Him a great big kiss!

All praise and glory be to the Lord!

CONTACT THE AUTHOR

You can contact the author via her website:
www.theendoftheworld.uk.com
and by e-mail: office@theendoftheworld.uk.com

You can also follow Michele on Facebook
via her website address above.

OTHER BOOKS BY THE AUTHOR

Come on Church! Wake Up!: Sin Within the Church and What Jesus Has to Say about It

Paperback: ISBN 978-1-62136-316-3
e-book: ISBN 978-1-62136-315-6

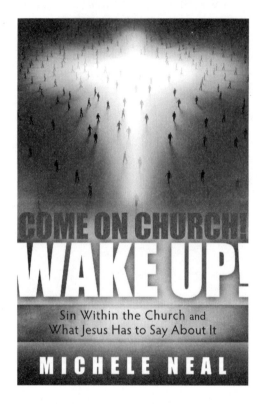

Website: www.comeonchurchwakeup.com
E-mail: info@comeonchurchwakeup.com

You can follow Michele on her Facebook page for this book via the website address above.